INSIGHT ⊙ GUIDES

EXPLORE

MADRID

⊙ Walking Eye App

YOUR FREE EBOOK AVAILABLE THROUGH THE WALKING EYE APP

Your guide now includes a free eBook to your chosen destination, for the same great price as before. Simply download the Walking Eye App from the App Store or Google Play to access your free eBook.

HOW THE WALKING EYE APP WORKS

Through the Walking Eye App, you can purchase a range of eBooks and destination content. However, when you buy this book, you can download the corresponding eBook for free. Just see below in the grey panel where to find your free content and then scan the QR code at the bottom of this page.

Destinations: Download essential destination content featuring recommended sights and attractions, restaurants, hotels and an A–Z of practical information, all available for purchase.

Ships: Interested in ship reviews? Find independent reviews of river and ocean ships in this section, all available for purchase.

eBooks: You can download your free accompanying digital version of this guide here. You will also find a whole range of other eBooks, all available for purchase.

Free access to travel-related blog articles about different destinations, updated on a daily basis.

HOW THE EBOOKS WORK

The eBooks are provided in EPUB file format. Please note that you will need an eBook reader installed on your device to open the file. Many devices come with this as standard, but you may still need to install one manually from Google Play.

The eBook content is identical to the content in the printed guide.

HOW TO DOWNLOAD THE WALKING EYE APP

1. Download the Walking Eye App from the App Store or Google Play.
2. Open the app and select the scanning function from the main menu.
3. Scan the QR code on this page – you will then be asked a security question to verify ownership of the book.
4. Once this has been verified, you will see your eBook in the purchased ebook section, where you will be able to download it.

Other destination apps and eBooks are available for purchase separately or are free with the purchase of the Insight Guide book.

CONTENTS

ARCHITECTURE

Trace Madrid's history from the Habsburg buildings around the Plaza Mayor (routes 2 and 3) to the flamboyant style of the early 20th-century on the Gran Vía (route 1) and the modern Paseo de la Castellana (route 12).

RECOMMENDED ROUTES FOR...

ART BUFFS

As well as the Thyssen-Bornemisza (route 4) Prado and Reina Sofía museums (route 5), don't miss the Real Academia de Bellas Artes de San Fernando (route 1) and the Lázaro Galdiano and Sorolla museums (route 12).

FAMILIES

Kids love the Natural Sciences museum and the Real Madrid stadium tour (route 12), as well as the Teleférico cable car, the zoo and the Parque de Atracciones funfair in the Casa de Campo (route 10).

FOODIES

Sample local delicacies and Spanish wines at the Mercado de San Miguel gourmet market, then eat at a traditional restaurant with a wood-fired oven or do a tapas crawl on Cava Baja (all route 2).

NIGHT OWLS

There are night spots to suit all tastes in the Malasaña and Chueca neighbourhoods (route 9), as well as in the streets around Plaza de Santa Ana (route 7).

ROMANCE

Make a special memory by watching the sunset at the Templo de Debod (route 10) or from a terrace table at Las Vistillas (route 3). Taking out a rowing boat in the Retiro Park can be pretty romantic too (route 6).

VIEWS

Take in the panoramic views from Centro Centro or the roof terrace at the Círculo de Bellas Artes (both route 1). Get even higher up at the Faro observation tower in Moncloa (route 11).

BACK TO NATURE

Breathe some fresh air in one of Madrid's green spaces. Stroll around the Retiro (route 6) or the Botanical Garden (route 5) and explore the Parque del Oeste (route 10) and the Casa de Campo (route 11).

INTRODUCTION

An introduction to Madrid's geography, customs and culture, plus illuminating background information on cuisine, history and what to do when you're there.

EXPLORE MADRID

Madrid is one of those places that just make people smile. With world–class museums, buzzing nightlife and a dynamic gastronomic scene, a visit to Spain's capital is sure to lift anyone's spirits.

Ask Madrilenians what they love most about their city and watch their eyes shine as they rave about the light and the vibrant atmosphere. Standing at an altitude of 667 metres (2,188 ft), Madrid is the highest major capital city in Europe, which may account for the dazzling light and the clear blue skies, but it is the people themselves who create the exhilarating energy that all visitors notice as soon as they arrive.

You could spend weeks in Madrid just visiting the top museums, such as the Prado, Thyssen-Bornemisza and Reina Sofía, but allow plenty of time for just drifting around the tapas bars too, which counts as a cultural experience in its own right in Madrid. This is a city where the best-laid plans are likely to be forgotten soon after the first cold beer at a pavement terrace.

Despite the severe economic problems that Spain has been going through in the last decade, the centre of Madrid has undergone a startling transformation, with shops, galleries and bars popping up everywhere in previously dilapidated downtown areas. Look up, however, and you'll invariably still see someone in their dressing-gown, quietly taking in the scene from a wrought-iron balcony while watering their plants.

GEOGRAPHY AND LAYOUT

Even though Madrid is a big capital city, it is surprisingly accessible with a compact central core. Wherever you stay, you can usually walk to the major museums and will often come across a lesser-known collection or gallery just around the corner – and there is nearly always an appealing tapas bar nearby too.

While it is by far the biggest city in Spain, most of the areas of interest to the visitor are concentrated around the city's core of the Puerta del Sol and are walkable for averagely-active people. Most of the routes in this book are less than five kilometres (3 miles), although striding around Madrid's many museums means you might cover a much greater distance.

If you follow route 1 on arrival, walking from the Puerta del Sol to the Gran Vía, you will get a good idea of the layout of the city. The oldest part of town, Madrid de los Austrias (see route 2), fans out west of the Puerta del Sol, around the Plaza Mayor. To the east is the charac-

terful Barrio de la Letras around Plaza de Santa Ana (see route 7), where many writers of the Golden Age lived. Now it is full of cafés and tapas bars. Immediately west of this area is the Paseo del Prado (see routes 4 and 5), the grand boulevard that was developed in the 18th century. Art lovers will be spending a lot of time walking up and down this stretch as they visit the three most important museums.

North of the Gran Vía, the narrow streets of Chueca, Malasaña and Conde Duque have a lively vibe with lots of cafés and interesting little shops. To get an idea of how the city has expanded, take a trip up the Paseo de la Castellana, veering off to the east into the large Salamanca district to find the city's best boutiques.

HISTORY

Compared to other European cities, Madrid is a young capital. Arabs from North Africa established a fortress in the 9th century, but Madrid only really got going when Felipe II chose it to be his capital in 1561 – moving the court from Toledo – because it was in a strategic position in the centre of Spain and the surrounding countryside was good for hunting.

While being named capital brought great wealth, it was helped enormously by this being Spain's Golden Age, with riches pouring in from the New World. This also led to the emergence of the first theatres and a lively cultural scene. The Bourbon monarch Car-

los III implemented far-reaching urban developments, which included the transformation of the Paseo del Prado into an elegant boulevard lined with educational institutions. One of these was a vast building that was intended to be devoted to natural sciences but instead became the Prado museum of art.

Upheavals in the 19th century culminated with the Spanish-American war of 1898, when Spain lost its last colonies of Cuba, Puerto Rico and the Philippines. This event had a profound effect on the mood of the nation and led to the creation of the intellectual movement known as the Generation of '98.

The 20th century brought the devastating Civil War from 1936 to 1939, followed by the dictatorship of General Franco, which lasted until his death in 1975. The freedom brought by his death in 1975 led to the explosion of creativity known as *la movida madrileña*, with filmmaker Pedro Almodóvar as its figurehead.

King Juan Carlos I, who had reigned since 1975 following the death of Franco, abdicated in 2014, allowing his son to become king as Felipe VI at the age of 46. Perceived to be more in touch with the mood of the nation, the new king and his family are very popular in the country and have brought about a renewed support for the monarchy.

CLIMATE

Colder than you might expect in winter and hotter than you would think possi-

Sunbathing in the Parque del Retiro

ble in summer, the Spanish capital has an extreme climate. Spring and autumn are very pleasant however – May, June, September and October are the most pleasant periods to visit. The hottest month is July, when the temperature can rise above 40°C (104°F). August is usually slightly cooler, particularly towards the end of the month. Madrilenians leave the city in droves from mid-July onwards, often staying away for a month or more. Despite the low temperatures in winter, the bright light and generally clear skies make this a good time to visit and the sunshine often warms the city up enough to sit outside during the day.

DON'T LEAVE MADRID WITHOUT...

Doing a tapas crawl. Some of the best food in the city comes in bite-sized portions. Drift from traditional tiled bars that have been going for a century or more to the sleek gastrobars where top chefs offer their creative cuisine in miniature form. See page 17.

Trying churros and chocolate. Eating churro fritters with a cup of gloopy hot chocolate in a traditional café is one of Madrid's most beloved customs. Although this calorific combo is most typical for breakfast, it goes down particularly well in the early hours after a night on the tiles. See page 41.

Walking around Madrid de los Austrias. Soak up the atmosphere of old Madrid by exploring the area around the Plaza Mayor, where the slate spires of the Habsburg period rise into the sky. At ground level, traditional taverns line the narrow streets. See page 32.

Visiting the museums on the Paseo del Arte. The Prado, Thyssen-Bornemisza, Reina Sofía and CaixaForum museums make this short stretch one of the best concentrations of art in the world. See the El Greco, Velázquez and Goya paintings at the Prado and Picasso's Guernica at the Reina Sofía. See pages 48 and 52.

Drinking vermouth. Having a vermouth with a tapa at about 1pm is a favourite Madrid custom. Pop into the Mercado de San Miguel or one of the bars on and around the Plaza Mayor or down the road on Cava Baja. See page 33.

Shopping on calle Fuencarral. For a cool shopping vibe, join the throng strolling up the pedestrianised calle Fuencarral from the Gran Vía, where the boutiques alternate with hip cafés and bars. See page 21.

Browsing the Rastro market. Hunt for a bargain at the sprawling flea market that spills down the hills below the Plaza Mayor on Sunday mornings. It is as much a social as a shopping expedition, with raucous tapas bars hidden behind the hundreds of stalls. See page 62.

Sauntering along the Gran Vía. Cutting through the centre of the city and brash and busy at all hours of the day and night, the Gran Vía is Madrid's most symbolic street. Look up as you walk along to appreciate the turrets and statues topping off the grandiose buildings. See page 30.

Guards at the Palacio Real

Bookshop on Pasadizo de San Ginés

January is the coldest month, when the temperature sometimes drops below 6°C (46°F). Although it rarely snows in the city, there is usually substantial snowfall in the Sierra de Guadarrama mountains to the northwest.

POPULATION

The city of Madrid has a population of 3.2 million, while a total of 6.5 million people live in the Madrid region – double the number of inhabitants in 1950. The average age for Spanish citizens is 44, while for foreign residents it is 35. The under 15s make up 14.4 percent of the inhabitants, while 20.5 percent are over 65 and 7.4 percent are over 80 years old – two thirds of them women.

Unlike some cities, there is no significant age difference in the various areas of Madrid. In downtown neighbourhoods such as Lavapiés, La Latina and Malasaña, communities of older people, many In flats they and their familles have occupied for decades, live alongside younger residents who have moved in to enjoy the advantages of living right in the centre.

Until the end of the 20th century, Madrid had a negligible number of citizens from other countries but now almost 400, 000 of the city inhabitants – 12.4 percent of the total – are from abroad. Most of the central neighbourhoods have a multicultural feel and this is particularly noticeable in Lavapiés (see page 63), where there are shops and restaurants catering to the Asian and Moroccan communities. More than a third of the foreign population is from Latin American countries, and around 110,000 inhabitants are from countries in the European Union, 46,000 of whom are Romanians.

El Rastro market is a social event

LOCAL CUSTOMS

With museums and shops open until at least 8pm, the afternoon drifts well into evening, giving people an extra chunk of time in the day. While 10pm is still the norm for dinner, there is a creeping trend towards eating earlier and many restaurants take reservations from

Bear and strawberry tree, symbol of Madrid, in the Puerta del Sol

9pm. Despite the late daily routine, with primetime television shows often ending after midnight, lots of Madrilenians start work at 9am and you need to be up early if you want to get anything done that involves bureaucracy or official organisations.

In summer, many people work what is known as a *jornada intensiva*, from 8am until 3pm, then finishing for the day. This means they can have a leisurely lunch, go to the pool or have a siesta – or maybe all three – before venturing back out when the temperature drops slightly in the evening.

While most shops and cultural centres in the city centre now open all day, smaller places still close for two or three hours in the afternoon.

POLITICS AND ECONOMICS

As the capital city, Madrid is the seat of the central government. Since 2011, the centre-right Partido Popular has been in power, led by prime minister Mariano Rajoy, who has managed to remain in post despite widespread corruption scandals and is now credited with leading Spain out of the recession that began in 2008. Unemployment is still among the highest in Europe however, particularly for young people.

Since 2015, the mayoress of the city has been Manuela Carmena, of Ahora Madrid (Madrid Now), an organisation that defines itself as a citizen

Plaza Mayor is lined with pavement cafés and tapas bars

platform of popular unity, rather than a conventional political party. Her ambitious programme of reforms is focused on improving the city's environmental situation with measures including traffic reduction and the promotion of cycling.

As well as the city council, Madrid has a regional government, led by Cristina Cifuentes of the Partido Popular.

TOP TIPS FOR VISITING MADRID

Late habits. Expect to do everything two hours later in Madrid. A lot of museums and shops do not open until 10am and close between 8pm and 10pm, which means you can pack a lot in. Locals have lunch at 2am and dinner at 10pm, while many bars do not liven up until after midnight.

Getting served. *Cuando puedas!* If you dread having to try and order in a frantic bar, just say this handy phrase with a wave of your hand. Pronounced *cwando pwet-haz*, it means 'when you've got a minute' and is a fool-proof way to attract a busy waiter's attention without sounding rude.

Tipping. Madrilenians leave very small tips in taxis, bars and restaurants, usually just a few coins and often nothing at all – but just leave whatever you feel comfortable with. In high-end places, however, international rules apply.

Paseo del Arte ticket. If you are planning to visit all three major museums – the Prado, Reina Sofía and Thyssen-Bornemisza – save 20 percent by buying this combined ticket, which is valid for a year, at the first one you go to (or purchase online in advance).

Free late admission. Some museums and monuments are free for the last two hours each day, including the Prado, the Reina Sofía and the Palacio Real, which is handy if you just want to see one section, or have another look at a particular work of art.

Quiet museums. While there are often queues to get into the big three art centres, there are rarely crowds in most of other museums in the city and you might even have the place to yourself. There is superb art in the Real Academia de Bellas Artes de San Fernando, Lazaro Galdiano and Cerralbo museums.

Bargain lunches. A lot of restaurants, whether basic or smart, offer a set-price deal at lunchtime. Aimed at workers rather than tourists, this usually comprises three courses and a drink and represents excellent value for money.

Shopping. Don't shop just in the streets around the Puerta del Sol. Head to Chueca, Malasaña, Conde Duque and the Barrio de las Letras for edgy independent shops and to the Salamanca area for smarter boutiques.

Beware of pickpockets. Madrid is a pretty safe city but cut down your chances of being robbed by keeping your essential belongings close to you and leave valuables in your hotel safe. Never leave a bag on the back of your chair in a café and be particularly vigilant in the metro.

Fresh seafood is superb in Madrid

FOOD AND DRINK

While the Spanish capital has the most exciting food scene in Spain and one of the best in Europe, classic dishes are more popular than ever, whether strictly traditional or with a creative contemporary update.

Traditional tapas or a gastrobar? Roast pork or tuna tataki? Madrilenians invest huge amounts of time and energy in eating and drinking in a mindboggling variety of forms. If you want to understand what makes the city tick, there is no better way of going about it than doing what the locals do – which means getting used to eating later than you might normally do, both for lunch and dinner.

It is surprising how many people think Spanish and Mexican food are pretty similar, when in fact they are poles apart. There are not that many spicy dishes in Spanish cooking, although chili peppers are used for some recipes, such as *gambas al ajillo* (prawns fried with chilli peppers, garlic and parsley).

While a lot of Spanish restaurants in other countries focus on tapas, in Madrid it is actually just as usual to go for a sit-down meal – although that might well involve sharing dishes, at least for the first course.

After decades of sticking stubbornly with the tried and tested, foreign influences are flooding into the city. A new generation of chefs and foodies is bringing fresh ideas to the table – literally – from what they have learned on their travels around the globe. This means juice bars, a trend towards healthier food and a much improved vegetarian scene. Spanish cuisine is not losing its essence, however, as chefs are using the experiences gained abroad to put a new spin on what is known as *la cocina de la abuela*, or grandmother's cooking, reinventing dishes to appeal to modern palates.

MADRILENIAN SPECIALITIES

Purists will be pleased to learn that traditional restaurants are still flourishing, priding themselves on the quality of their roast meats, particularly lamb and suckling pig, which are cooked in huge wood-burning ovens.

Madrid's most characteristic dish is not paella but *cocido madrileño*, a robust stew that has evolved from the *olla podrida* and the Jewish *adafina* of medieval times. Made with chickpeas, pork, beef, chorizo sausage, cabbage, leeks, noodles and quite a few more things too, it is served in stages: first the broth with vermicelli in it, then the various vegetables and finally the meats and sausages. Another speciality is *callos a la madrileña*, which is tripe cooked

Traditional tapas dishes   *Do try the roast lamb*

in a tomato sauce with *pimentón*, the Spanish version of paprika. Both are more suited to winter, as is *sopa castellana*, a warming soup made with the simplest of ingredients: meat stock, garlic, bread, *pimentón* paprika and eggs.

Madrid may be hundreds of kilometres from the sea but fish and seafood are superb, having been transported in refrigerated trucks or planes from the Atlantic and the Mediterranean. Madrilenians love bream and hake, while one of the most typical things to eat in the city is the *bocadillo de calamares*, a chunky roll stuffed with squid rings in batter.

Tapas

To do things properly, tapas should ideally be consumed standing up and shared between two or more people. Order a couple of tapas at each place, with a beer or a glass of wine, then move on somewhere else, going to at least three or four in an evening.

A tapa is usually a very small portion. If you are sharing between several people, order a *media ración* or a *ración*. Just look around at what other people are having and don't be afraid to ask them what it is – that is all part of the fun. It is not obligatory to move from place to place, however. Most places have tables and if you are comfortable where you are, just stay put.

WHERE TO EAT

With a few days in Madrid, you could have a meal at a classic restaurant, eat at a few informal places with modern cuisine and have a couple of evenings on a tapas crawl down Cava Baja or around Plaza Santa Ana. Provided you are not too fussy, do as the Madrilenians do and have a set-price lunch wherever you happen to be.

Traditional restaurants

If you like good quality, no-nonsense food, be sure to have a meal at one of the restaurants near the Plaza Mayor. While **Botín** (see page 99) is the most famous – and the oldest – **Casa Lucío** (see page 37) is a good option, as is **Los Galayos** (see page 99). While these all specialise in roast suckling pig and lamb, there are plenty of other options on the menu if that is not your thing.

Tapas bars

There is quite a contrast between the tapas bars that have been around for decades and the more modern gastro-bars, which started emerging in the late 1990s and are now an established part of the gastronomic scene. Try traditional tapas at **El Lacón** (see page 101), **La Bodega de la Ardosa** (see page 103) or **Bocaíto** (see page 103). For a more contemporary vibe, grab a stool at **Angelita** (see page 102) or **La Dichosa** (see page 103).

Modern Spanish restaurants

Madrid is particularly strong on less formal places where the focus is on the fresh flavours and less fuss. With a younger

San Miguel market was one of the first gourmet markets

vibe and pared-back décor, these restaurants are usually run by talented young chefs with creative ideas and are often excellent value. **La Vinoteca de Moratín**

Gourmet markets

In the last decade, a different sort of market has been emerging all over Madrid. Some are revamps of existing food markets, while others are totally new. Some mix fruit and vegetable stalls with tapas bars, others are more like gastronomic food courts. All are dynamic spaces where visitors can taste all sorts of local produce as well as wines from all over the country. You just graze around the stalls picking up what you fancy then find yourself a table.

The trend was kick-started by the Mercado de San Miguel (see page 33), which opened in 2009 by the Plaza Mayor. While the Mercado de Antón Martín (calle Santa Isabel 5, www.mercadoantonmartin.com) is still very much a local market, now sushi and smoothies are on offer too. The Mercado de San Ildefonso (calle Fuencarral 57; mercadodesanildefonso.com), between fashionable Chueca and Malasaña, is packed out in the evenings and at weekends. Nearby, the Mercado de San Antón (see page 67) combines tapas places and deli stalls with a great restaurant and a groovy bar up on the roof terrace. Originally a cinema, Platea (see page 78) is where well-groomed Madrilenians take a break from the designer boutiques on nearby Serrano street.

(see page 53) and **Triciclo** (see page 102) are good options.

Michelin stars

There are 18 Michelin-starred restaurants in the Madrid region, but David Muñoz is the only chef to have won three stars. Eating at his restaurant **DiverXo** (see page 105), where the astonishing cuisine mixes Spanish and Asian influences, is as much a theatrical as a gastronomic experience. Muñoz also runs the **StreetXo** bar at **Gourmet Experience** (see page 105), where anyone can try his zingy dishes if they don't mind queuing.

The six restaurants with two Michelin stars include **Ramon Freixa Madrid** (see page 105) and Paco Roncero's **La Terraza del Casino** (see page 99). Eight places have one star, including **Punto MX** (see page 105), which serves spectacular Mexican food.

DRINKS

Wine

Madrilenians are remarkably unsnobbish about wine, but that may be because the quality is so great and the prices so reasonable. Many bars sell a good range by the glass, and this is a perfect opportunity to try reds from wine regions such as Ribera del Duero, El Bierzo or Priorat and whites from Rueda, Rias Baixas or Alella. You should also try wines made in the Madrid region, such as those from the organic winery Bodega Saavedra in Cenicientos in the southwest of

Typical bars serve locally brewed and craft beers

the region. In warm weather a refreshing choice is *tinto de verano*, which is simply red wine topped up with lemonade over lots of ice in a long glass. This is much more popular than *sangría*, which is also usually available at pavement cafés.

Vermouth

Something you really should get our head around in Madrid is the *hora del aperitivo*. This is the hour, sometime after noon and before lunch, that the Madrilenians like to devote to having a civilised drink, preferably the local red vermouth, although beer and wine are acceptable too, accompanied by a few tasty bites to sharpen up the appetite. Although it never really went away, vermouth is very much in fashion. Vermut Zarro is made in Madrid and is often available on draught in bars and restaurants.

Beer

Lager-style beer is tremendously popular, particularly Mahou, which is brewed in Madrid. Locals usually ask for a *caña*, which is a small glass of draught beer. If you want something bigger, ask for a doble. Craft beers are increasingly common, with several brewed in or around the city. Look out for Cervezas La Vírgen.

Mixed drinks

Madrilenians are very keen on their *copas*, as mixed drinks are known, and are frankly fanatical about gin and tonics, which are often served in huge balloon glasses. It is important to always state the brand of gin, whisky, vodka or whatever that you want – and see it poured in front of you – otherwise you might be served one of dubious quality.

Coffee

Coffee is invariably made in an espresso machine, usually using high-roast beans. Asking for *un café* or *un solo* will get you a straight espresso. *Café con leche* is a shot of espresso with about twice the quantity of hot milk. *Un cortado* is espresso with just a dash of hot milk. A *carajillo* is black coffee with a slug of brandy (or whatever you prefer).

Soft drinks

A wide range of non-alcoholic drinks is available, including beer, which is *cerveza sin alcohol*. Surprisingly, orange juice is not always fresh, so specify *natural* when ordering. In summer, try a *granizado de limón* – lemon juice blended with crushed ice and sugar – or *horchata*, a concoction of *chufas*, the tubers grown in the Valencia region that are known as tiger nuts, and also mixed with crushed ice and sugar.

Food and Drink Prices

The price guide is based on a two-course meal with one glass of wine:
€€€€ = more than 60 euros
€€€ = 40–60 euros
€€ = 25–40 euros
€ = less than 25 euros

A colourful display of fans at Casa Diego

SHOPPING

While Spanish brands seem to be taking over high streets all over Europe and beyond, there is a lot more to shopping in Madrid than the familiar names, with independent boutiques and traditional shops all over town.

WHAT TO BUY

Department stores sit alongside tiny shops that just sell umbrellas, espadrilles or gloves in the centre of Madrid, where shopping is an activity to be enjoyed rather than endured. Spain has a long tradition of making good-quality shoes and bags and there is a wide range of both classic and contemporary

Leather sandals at El Rastro market

designs on offer. Expect to pay for high prices for handmade items, however.

Gourmet foods make good gifts and are widely available at specialist shops, department stores and gastronomic markets (see page 18). Look out for *pimentón* paprika in pretty tins, olive oil, sherry vinegar, *turrón* nougat and chocolates. *Ibérico* ham, *chorizo* and other charcuterie, as well as cheeses, can usually be vaccum packed.

While larger stores and boutiques stay open all day – including Sundays – usually from 9.30am until 8.30pm, small shops close from 2pm to 5pm. All over the city, you will have no difficulty finding convenience stores that sell mineral water as well as other drinks and snacks.

WHERE TO BUY

Around the Puerta del Sol and Gran Vía

The pedestrianised area between the Puerta del Sol and the Gran Vía, formed by calle Preciados and adjoining streets, is packed with mainstream clothes and shoe shops, such as Zara, Mango and Camper, and this is where the original branch of El Corte Inglés

The bustling shopping street, calle Fuencarral

department store is situated. Fnac (calle Preciados 28) is a very useful store for books (including in English), music and any bits and pieces you might need for your phone or camera. The Casa del Libro (Gran Vía 29) is a huge bookshop with an English section and a wide variety of guidebooks and books on Madrid. Casa Diego (Puerta del Sol 12) has been in business since 1858 and specialises in handmade fans. Nearby at calle Cruz 23, Capas Seseña has been making capes for more than a century.

Around the Plaza Mayor and Madrid de los Austrias

The Austrias neighbourhood behind the Plaza Mayor around calle Toledo has the densest concentration of traditional old shops with wooden frontages and painted glass signs, but these are sadly disappearing fast. For a huge range of traditional espadrilles and a mind-boggling array of other rope-related items, don't miss Casa Hernanz (calle Toledo 18). For classic hats and shawls, browse around the porticoed galleries of the Plaza Mayor.

Calle Serrano and Salamanca area

The smartest shops are in the grid of streets in the Salamanca district, where all the well-known chain stores are also present. Calle Serrano and calle Goya both have an upmarket high street feel, while Claudio Coello, Lagasca and Jorge Juan streets are quieter but also packed with boutiques. On calle Serrano, look out for Manolo Blahnik, who was born in La Palma in the Canary Islands and has an elegant shop at No. 58. Ágatha Ruíz de La Prada, one of Spain's best known designers, has her shop at No. 27, with brightly coloured clothes for adults and children. Calle José Ortega y Gasset is lined with top international names, such as Christian Dior (No. 6), and Chanel (No. 14). Lavinia (No. 16) is a fabulous wine shop with a gastrobar upstairs. The Mercado de la Paz (calle Ayala 28) is a great food market with delicatessen stalls.

Around calle Fuencarral

The pedestrianised street is lined with shops, including Desigual, Muji and Mac. Calle Augusto Figueroa, which is known for its outlet shoe shops, runs through Chueca to the Salesas area, where Barquillo, Almirante and Conde de Xiquena are the streets to explore for upmarket independent boutiques.

In Malasaña, the liveliest streets for shopping are Corredera Alta de San Pablo, Espíritu Santo, Manuela Malasaña and cross streets. At calle Divino Pastor No. 29, family-run Antigua Casa Crespo was founded in 1865 and specialises in espadrilles of every description.

In the lower part of the neighbourhood, nearer the Gran Vía, Madrilenian hipsters hunt for vintage treasures in the edgier Triball area, trawling the boutiques and galleries on Valverde and Pez streets.

A well-attended corrida in the prestigious Las Ventas bullring

ENTERTAINMENT

Madrid nightlife is hectic, fast-moving and carries on all night. Gregarious at heart, Madrilenians are night creatures, hopping in and out of tabernas, restaurants and bars. But they are also a sophisticated bunch, and cultural distractions are plentiful.

It often seems that the entire population is on the streets after dark in Madrid. Every night there is a huge range of theatre, music and dance events to choose from, with something to suit all tastes and budgets. Throughout the summer, there are performances at outdoor venues all over the city, often at very reasonable prices.

While you usually need to book ahead for the opera or major concerts, for the majority of events you can buy tickets on the day or just turn up. An easy way to find out what is on is to look at the What's On section of the Madrid tourism website, www.esmadrid.es. Information on individual venues is given in the Nightlife section (see page 106).

THEATRE

Madrid's theatre tradition can be traced back to the Golden Age in the 17th century (see page 58). Classic and contemporary Spanish plays are still performed in the same area as the original courtyard venues, at the Teatro Nacional (see page 58) and the Teatro de la Comedia (calle Príncipe 14), as well as at the Teatro María Guerrero (calle Tamayo y Beus 4), which is the home of the Centro Dramático Nacional (National Dramatic Centre).

Once the Broadway of Madrid, the Gran Vía has lost a lot of its theatres, but several on the stretch from Plaza de Callao to Plaza de España are still going strong by staging major musicals, such as *The Lion King* or *The Phantom of the Opera*.

CLASSICAL MUSIC AND OPERA

While it is a very special experience to see an opera or a concert at the magnificent Teatro Real (see page 40), it is also interesting to see the more typically Madrilenian form of light opera, known as *zarzuela*, whether at the Teatro de la Zarzuela (see page 106) or in one of the city's parks or gardens in summer. The main venue for classical music is the splendid Auditorio Nacional de Música (see page 106), with regular concerts by Spanish and international orchestras and performers.

JAZZ, ROCK AND POP

There is a variety of live music every night in the city, whether large-scale concerts

Choose from a variety of bars in the old town for after-dinner drinks

by major artists or more intimate events in small theatres, cultural centres and clubs. Throughout the summer months individual concerts and festivals are held outdoors too, often in magical settings. A jazz festival is staged in November at the Centro Cultural Conde Duque (see page 67), where there are regular concerts of all sorts of music.

DANCE

Madrid has a dynamic dance scene, ranging from classical to contemporary. The Ballet Nacional de España, which focuses on Spanish styles, and the more experimental Compañía Nacional de Danza perform at several theatres, including the Teatro Real. The Víctor Ullate Ballet – Comunidad de Madrid company is based at the Teatros del Canal. Other key venues include the Teatro Albéniz, the Teatro Fernán Gómez (see page 75) and the Matadero cultural centre.

FLAMENCO

While Andalucía is the home of flamenco, its best exponents perform regularly in Madrid, giving visitors a chance to experience both the traditional and contemporary versions of this extraordinary art. It can be tricky as a visitor to find truly authentic flamenco, as the best tend to be both unplanned and private, but the city has several venues run by flamenco artists where you can see top-quality musicians and dancers (see page 107).

BULLFIGHTING

Bullfighting continues to be an important part of Spanish life. Although many Spaniards do not support it, the *aficionados* are fiercely passionate about not just the fights themselves but the whole culture surrounding the activity. Madrid's main bullring, Las Ventas, is one of the largest and most prestigious in the world. The season runs from March to October, but the most exciting periods, with top matadors appearing every evening, are the San Isidro festival in May and the Otoño (Autumn) festival at the end of September.

NIGHTLIFE

Nightlife is just life in Madrid, as this is a city where staying out late is the norm rather than the exception. If you just go out for dinner and a drink or two afterwards you will be lucky to get to bed before 2am. Any time before that is regarded as an early night. Going out is not restricted to millennials either – you see people of all ages enjoying a drink with friends in both the most traditional and the most fashionable bars.

Lively areas at night include Plaza de Santa Ana, Malasaña and La Latina (around Cava Baja and Plaza de la Paja). A lot of bars have to close at 2am – regulations are very strict – but there is no shortage of places that open later.

HISTORY: KEY DATES

While its origins as a Muslim settlement by the Manzanares river were humble, Madrid started growing fast after becoming the capital of Spain in the mid–16th century, acquiring the dynamic character that survives to this day.

EARLY HISTORY

852	The Emir of Córdoba, Mohammed I, builds the Alcázar fortress where the Almudena cathedral is now.
1085	Alfonso VI conquers Toledo and captures the fortress from the Muslims after a three-year siege in 1086.
1202	Alfonso VIII grants Madrid its own *fuero* (statutes), formalising town laws and rights.
1309	Fernando IV holds the first parliament in Madrid.
1369	The foundation of the Trastamara dynasty consolidates Madrid's position with the embellishment of the Alcázar.
1465	Enrique IV gives Madrid the title 'very noble and very loyal'.
1474	Rule of the Catholic Monarchs, Isabel I of Castile and Fernando of Aragón.
1492	Jews expelled; Christopher Columbus discovers the New World in the name of Spain.

HABSBURG MADRID AND THE GOLDEN AGE

1516	The Habsburg period begins when Carlos I, Holy Roman Emperor, is crowned king of Spain.
1561	Felipe II establishes capital in Madrid, replacing Toledo.
1563	Building of El Escorial begins.
1547	Birth of the writer Miguel de Cervantes.
1601–06	Madrid renamed capital after brief stint in Valladolid.
1617–19	Construction of the Plaza Mayor.
1621–65	Reign of Felipe IV.
1623	Diego de Velázquez is appointed court painter.
1625	Work begins on the fourth and final city wall, demolished in 1860.
1632	The Buen Retiro Palace is built.

Goya's The San Isidro Meadow (1788) – a panoramic view of Madrid

BOURBON MADRID

1701–14	War of Spanish Succession; start of the Bourbon rule.
1738	Construction of the royal palace begins on the site of the Alcázar.
1746	Birth of the painter Francisco Goya.
1752	Foundation of the Real Academia de Bellas Artes de San Fernando; reign of Fernando VI.
1759–88	Reign of Carlos III, the 'mayor-king'; major urban development.
1808	Carlos IV abdicates; Madrid revolts against the French army.
1808–14	Peninsula War; Joseph Bonaparte becomes king.
1814–33	Reign of Fernando VII.
1819	The Prado museum opens.
1836	State confiscation; demolition of monasteries and convents in city centre.
1851	First train service from Madrid to Aranjuez.
1874	Restoration of the Bourbon monarchy.

20TH CENTURY

1919	The metro underground system opens.
1931–36	Abdication of Alfonso XIII; start of the Second Republic.
1936–39	Spanish Civil War.
1939–75	Dictatorship of General Francisco Franco.
1975	Juan Carlos I is crowned King of Spain.
1979	Enrique Tierno Galván is elected mayor of Madrid and La Movida creative movement emerges.
1981	Colonel Tejero storms the parliament building in a failed military coup.
1986	Spain joins the European Union.

21ST CENTURY

2004	Terrorist attack on commuter trains results in 201 deaths.
2011	The Indignados movement occupies the Puerta del Sol, protesting against unemployment, corruption and the establishment.
2014	King Juan Carlos I abdicates and his son becomes king as Felipe VI.
2015	Manuela Carmena of the Ahora Madrid (Madrid Now) citizen platform becomes mayoress.
2017	The Spanish government, based in Madrid, clamps down on Catalonia's bid for independence.

BEST ROUTES

PUERTA DEL SOL
AND THE GRAN VÍA

*Tracing the triangle from the Puerta del Sol along Calle de Alcalá and back
along the Gran Vía, this short route through the core of the city helps you get
your bearings and includes some of Madrid's best-known landmarks.*

DISTANCE: 2.5km (1.5 miles)
TIME: 2 hours
START/END: Puerta del Sol
POINTS TO NOTE: This easy walk is good
to do on arrival and combines well with
routes 2, 7 and 9. Beware of pickpockets
in the Puerta del Sol and along the Gran
Vía, which are always crowded.

The Puerta del Sol is the central point of
the city. Walking along calle de Alcalá,
you see examples of the grand architectural style of the late 19th and early 20th
centuries. Many were originally banks,
illustrating how Madrid developed com-
mercially in that period. Nowadays,
these streets are lined with shops and
cafés, and a few cultural institutions too.

PUERTA DEL SOL

Ten streets converge on the **Puerta del
Sol ❶** – locals call it simply Sol – which
is the heart of Madrid and has one of the
city's busiest metro stations. The name
means Gate of the Sun and comes from

the eastern gate in the 15th-century city
wall. While the city's intellectuals used
to meet at cafés here, now most people
are just rushing through the semicircular
space, clutching bags from the shops in
the surrounding streets. People do con-
gregate here, however, for protests and
demonstrations, and it is most crowded
on New Year's Eve, when Madrilenians
gather for the ritual of eating a grape
with each chime as the clock strikes
midnight to bring them good luck.

Casa de Correos

The red-brick clock tower crowns the
Casa de Correos, built in 1768 as the
central post office and now holds the
headquarters of the regional government.
The popular uprising against Napoleon's
army took place in front of the building on
2 May 1808. The following day, hundreds
of people were shot here in cold blood, a
scene immortalised by Goya.

Kilómetro Cero

Look down at the pavement in front of
the building, where a semicircular plaque
marks "Kilometre Zero", the official cen-

The Puerta del Sol, Madrid's busiest square

tre of Spain: distances to everywhere in the country are measured from this point.

El Oso y Madroño

The most popular feature in the Puerta del Sol is the bronze statue of a bear jumping up at an arbutus (or wild strawberry) tree, which is Madrid's most famous – and most photographed – symbol and features on the city's coat of arms.

The equestrian statue on the curving north side is of King Carlos III and is a relatively recent addition (1997).

CALLE DE ALCALÁ

Stretching east from the Puerta del Sol, calle de Alcalá originated as the cere-monial royal route to the historic town of Alcalá de Henares, 35km (22 miles) away. At the turn of the 20th century, the street was Madrid's financial hub, which led to the construction of ostentatious banking headquarters.

REAL ACADEMIA DE BELLAS ARTES DE SAN FERNANDO

On the left at No. 13 is the **Real Academia de Bellas Artes de San Fernando** ❷ (Royal Academy of Fine Arts of San Fernando; www.rabasf.com; Tue–Sun 10am–3pm; free Wed). Founded in the 18th century, this museum attracts surprisingly few visitors given the importance of its displays. There are 13 paintings by

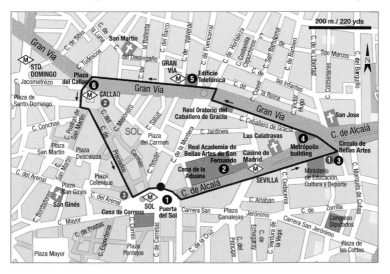

Goya, including *The Burial of the Sardine* and two self-portraits, as well as works by El Greco, Zurbarán, Rubens and Picasso.

The opulent building next door at No. 15 is the **Casino de Madrid**, built in 1910. While this is a private club, anyone can book a table at La Terraza restaurant on the top floor, where chef Paco Roncero holds two Michelin stars (see page 99).

Up ahead on the right, on the corner of calle Sevilla, raise your gaze to see two chariots, each drawn by four horses, which seem to be galloping into the sky. On the left is the 17th-century Baroque church of **Las Calatravas** (Mon–Sun 9am–12.15pm, 6pm–7.15pm; free), with an ornate altarpiece by José Benito de Churriguera.

CÍRCULO DE BELLAS ARTES

On the right at No. 42 stands the **Círculo de Bellas Artes** ❸ (Fine Arts Circle; www. circulobellasartes.com; exhibition areas Tue–Sun 11am–2pm, 5–9pm), a popular cultural centre that was designed by Antonio Palacios in 1920. Zoom up to the Azotea roof terrace for panoramic views (Mon–Fri 9am–2am, Sat–Sun 11am–2am). **La Pecera** café, see ❶, on the ground floor is a good place for a coffee.

Further down the street, you can see Plaza de Cibeles (see page 44) with the Puerta de Alcalá on the hill beyond (see page 54).

The **Metrópolis** ❹ building stands at the apex of the chevron-shaped junction of calle Alcalá and the Gran Vía.

Designed by Jules and Raymond Février between 1907 and 1910, it has a striking façade with a bronze figure of the Winged Victory on top of the slate dome.

Crossing to the north side of the junction, admire the **Iglesia de San José** (Mon–Sun 7am–1pm, 6pm–9pm; free), which dates back to the 1730s and was designed by Pedro de Ribera.

GRAN VÍA

The capital's most famous street was developed in three stages in the first half of the 20th century. In the early years, people flocked there to admire the grand buildings, go to the theatres and stop off at the fashionable cafés. Nowadays, you will see more chain boutiques and fast-food joints, but it still teems with life at all hours.

The curved, colonnaded façade of the Grassy jeweller's heralds the beginning of the avenue. In this first section, you see how the architects were keen to emulate the elegant Paris boulevards created by Haussmann. On the right at No. 12 is the legendary **Museo Chicote** cocktail bar (see page 107), which dates back to the 1930s.

Oratorio del Caballero de Gracia

On the left at No. 17 is the curving rear façade of the restored **Real Oratorio del Caballero de Gracia** (entrance on parallel calle Caballero de Gracia; Mon–Sun 10am–1.45pm, 5pm–8.45pm; free). Designed by Juan de Villanueva at the end of the 18th century, it is one of the

Gran Vía and calle Alcalá crossroads at dusk

best examples of neoclassical architecture in the city.

The junction with Montera, Hortaleza and Fuencarral streets marks the start of the second section of the Gran Vía, which was built in the 1920s. The architecture on this stretch combines Art Deco features with the American influences.

The Telefónica Building

The massive structure on the right is the **Edificio Telefónica ❺** headquarters of Spain's main telecommunications' company. Madrid's first skyscraper, it is 88 metres (289 ft) tall and was designed by the American architect Louis S. Weeks. It also houses the **Fundación Telefónica** (https://espacio.fundaciontelefonica. com; Tue–Sun 10am–8pm), which has an outstanding art collection (entrance at calle Fuencarral 3).

Shops have replaced most of the cinemas and theatres that characterised the avenue until the first decade of the 21st century. Join the crowds walking along to the **Plaza del Callao ❻**. The curved Art Deco façade up ahead is the Carrión building by Martínez Fecuchi y Vicente Eced, which houses the Capitol hotel and cinema. For a drink with a view of the Gran Vía rooftops, go up to **Gourmet Experience**, see ❷, on the top floor of **El Corte Inglés** department store.

Calle Preciados

Turn left down calle Preciados which leads back down to the Puerta del Sol. After passing another large El Corte Inglés, turn right into calle Tetuán to reach **Casa Labra** tapas bar, see ❸, which is an excellent place to end your walk.

Food and Drink

❶ LA PECERA

Círculo de Bellas Artes, Calle Alcalá 42; tel: 91 3605400; www.lapeceradelcirculo.com; Mon–Thu 8am–1am, Fri–Sun 8am–3am; €
This grand café, decorated with chandeliers, paintings and a marble statue, is an impressive place for breakfast or a drink, snack or meal at any time, as you watch the world go by from a window table.

❷ GOURMET EXPERIENCE

El Corte Inglés, Plaza de Callao 2; tel: 91 379800; www.elcorteingles.es/ supermercado/aptc/gourmet-experience/ granvia; Mon–Sun 10am–midnight; €
This food court on the 9th floor of the department store has a variety of food and drink outlets to suit all tastes, as well as speciality foods that make good gifts.

❸ CASA LABRA

Calle Tetuán 12; tel: 91 5310081; www.casalabra.es; Mon–Sat 9.30am–3.30pm, 5.30pm–11pm; €
Established in 1860, this traditional tavern is where Pablo Iglesias founded the Spanish Socialist Workers' Party (PSOE) in 1879. The most popular tapas are the cod strips in batter and the *croquetas*. The draught beer is very good here too.

PLAZA MAYOR AND MADRID DE LOS AUSTRIAS

Madrid de Los Austrias – or Habsburg Madrid – is the oldest part of the city. While not many buildings survive from the medieval period, it is easy to trace the capital's history in the narrow streets, which are still full of character.

DISTANCE: 2.5km (1.5 miles)
TIME: 3 hours
START: Plaza Mayor
END: Plaza de Santa Cruz
POINTS TO NOTE: You could do this route in the morning, visiting the museums and churches, then again in the evening, going to tapas bars along the way. The streets are very atmospheric at dusk.

The Habsburgs reigned from 1561, when Madrid became the capital of Spain, to 1700. This was the Golden Age, when Madrid was the headquarters of the Spanish Empire following the discovery of the Americas.

PLAZA MAYOR

You can soak up 400 years of history in the **Plaza Mayor ❶**. Framed by elegant red-brick buildings with slate roofs and spindly spires – the traditional Habsburg architectural features – the elegant square may no longer be the hub of city life that it once was, but it is still used for all sorts of events, including a Christmas market. Pavement cafés sprawl across the cobbles and tapas bars and traditional shops line the arcades.

Designed by Juan Gómez de Mora in 1617, over time it has been used for bullfights, as a theatre for plays by Golden Age writers, jousting and the sinister trials known as *autos-da-fe*, held by the Inquisition. The height of the buildings was revolutionary at the time and housed around 3,000 citizens, inspiring jokes about people living on top of each other.

Following a fire at the end of the 18th century, the square was redesigned by Juan de Villanueva, the architect of the Prado Museum, who added the entrance arches and made the buildings the same height. The equestrian statue of Felipe III in the middle of the square was made in the 17th century by Giovanni de Bologna and Pietro Tacca but not installed here until the mid-19th century.

The frescoes on the north side of the square were created relatively recently, in 1992, by Carlos Franco, and decorate the building known as the Casa de

Plaza Mayor, an architectural symphony of bold but balanced lines

la Panaderia, originally the headquarters of the bakers' guild. Nowadays, the ground floor houses the city's main tourist information centre.

MERCADO DE SAN MIGUEL

Leave the Plaza Mayor through the arch in the northwestern corner, walking along calle Ciudad Rodrigo. Calle Cava San Miguel to the left is lined with traditional tapas bars, but leave them for the evening and instead look straight ahead, where people will be streaming in and out of the **Mercado de San Miguel**, see ❶. The dainty ironwork structure, which dates back to 1916, housed a neighbourhood market for nearly a century – until it was turned into a gastronomic hub in

2009. An instant success, it was the catalyst for the trend for gourmet markets in Madrid and indeed throughout Spain.

PLAZA DE LA VILLA

Walk along calle Mayor to the elegant **Plaza de la Villa ❷**, which was the most important square in medieval Madrid. The 17th-century **Casa de la Villa** (on the right looking from the calle Mayor) is one of the key buildings of Habsburg Madrid and was designed by Juan Gómez de Mora. Until 2007 it housed the City Hall, which then moved to the Palacio de Cibeles (see page 45). Opposite is the **Torre y Casa de los Lujanes**, dating back to the time of the Catholic Monarchs in the late 15th-cen-

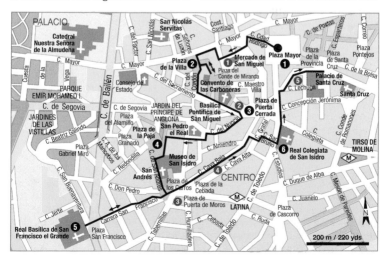

Stalls at the San Miguel market

tury. The main door in Gothic style was added in the 1920s, but the arch on the right is the work of Mudéjar artisans.

If you walk down the narrow calle del Codo – meaning 'elbow' in Spanish and curves around the building – you come to the Plaza del Conde de Miranda, with the 17th-century **Convento de las Carboneras** on the right (10am–1pm, 4–7pm; free), which gets its name from an image of the Virgin that was found in a coal yard. The nuns make and sell their own cakes, which you can buy by means of a rotating drum called a *torno* – this is a closed order so the nuns cannot be seen.

Returning to the Plaza de la Villa, at the bottom of the square is the Plateresque **Casa de Cisneros**, built in the 16th century for the nephew of Cardinal Cisneros and remodelled in the early 20th century.

BASÍLICA PONTÍFICA DE SAN MIGUEL

Cut down the side of the building to **calle Sacramento**, one of the best preserved streets in Madrid. Turning left, the street becomes calle San Justo, with the **Basílica Pontífica de San Miguel** (www.bsmiguel.es; Mon–Sat 9.45am–1.30pm, 5.30–9.15pm, Sun 9.45am–2.15pm, 6–9.15pm; free) on the left, which now belongs to the Opus Dei organisation. Built in the mid-18th century, the Baroque church features circular vaults over the single nave. Also from that period is the **Palacio Arzobispal** (Archbishop's Palace) next door.

PLAZA DE PUERTA CERRADA

You come out at the **Plaza de Puerta Cerrada ❸**, the site of another medieval city gate but now better known for its striking murals, added in the 1980s by Alberto Corazón. A few traditional shops survive in and around the square, a vestige of the muleteers and wagon-drivers who came from every region to sell their wares and buy tools and supplies such as sieves and ropes. On the left at No. 11 is the brightly-painted wooden façade of **Casa Paco**, see ❷, one of the city's most traditional taverns.

Cross over calle Segovia at the traffic lights and turn into the narrow calle del Nuncio, which is lined with palatial residences, now mostly official buildings. At the end you come upon the **Iglesia de San Pedro el Viejo** (Mon–Thu 9am–12.30pm, 5–8pm, Fri 7am–8pm, Sat 9am–12.30pm, 5–8pm, Sun 9am–12.30pm; free), founded in the mid-14th century but largely rebuilt in the 17th century. The brick tower with loophole windows is one of the few examples of Mudéjar architecture in Madrid.

PLAZA DE LA PAJA

Walk down the pedestrianised calle Príncipe de Anglona to the **Plaza de la Paja ❹**. At the end of the street and the bottom of the square, is the **Jardín del Príncipe de Anglona** (summer 10am–10pm, winter 10am–6.30pm; free) a tiny yet delightful garden created

Plaza de la Villa

The delightful Jardín del Príncipe de Anglona

in the 18th century and laid out in its current form in 1920.

The sloping Plaza de la Paja looks calm now, with its café terraces under the trees, but in Moorish times this was the heart of Madrid and in the Middle Ages the wealthiest families lived in palaces around the square.

Workers from the fields down by the river had to donate a 10th of their crop to the **Iglesia de San Andrés** (Mon–Sat 9am–1pm, 6–8pm, Sun 9am–1pm; free), which dominates the top of the space (entrance on Plaza de San Andrés). The church was founded in the 13th century and was rebuilt in the 17th century before being severely damaged by fire in the Civil War.

The part of the structure giving onto the square is the late-Gothic **Capilla del Obispo** (Mon–Fri 6pm–8pm, Sat–Sun noon–1.30pm; free) with its extraordinarily ornate Plateresque decoration.

THE SQUARE WITH FOUR NAMES

Walking out of the square around the side of the church brings you to a space that has four different names: this part is **Plaza de los Carros**, after the wagons and stagecoaches that used to arrive here from Toledo and all around Spain. To the south it is the **Puerta de Moros**, after a city gate that stood here, while in the middle it is the **Plaza del Humilladero**. By the entrance to the church, it is the **Plaza de San Andrés**. There are lots of pavement cafés and restaurants

in the square, including **Juana La Loca**, see ❸, where you can have a drink with a tapa or a sit-down meal.

MUSEO DE SAN ISIDRO

Just beyond the church on Plaza de San Andrés the **Museo de San Isidro** (www.madrid.es/museosanisidro; Tue–Sun 9.30am–8pm, mid-June–mid-Sept 10am–7pm; free) charts Madrid's origins from prehistoric times until the establishment of the court in the 16th century and gives an overview of how the city developed over the centuries. The Museo de la Historia de Madrid (see page 65) deals with later periods in Madrid's history.

It is claimed that Madrid's patron saint, San Isidro Labrador (St Isidore the Labourer), lived in a house on this site and the final section of the displays deals with his life and the many miracles he performed (see box page 36). Fragments remain from the 16th and 17th centuries, including the Renaissance courtyard and the chapel.

REAL BASÍLICA DE SAN FRANCISCO EL GRANDE

From the square, you could make a short detour down Carrera de San Francisco to see the **Real Basílica de San Francisco el Grande** ❺ (Tue–Sun 10.30am–1pm, 5–7.30pm; guided tour), one of the most important churches in the city.

Legend has it that St. Francis of Assisi founded a chapel here in 1217.

The curving calle Cava Baja

This much grander structure was built in the mid-18th century, although construction was beset by problems owing to the massive dome, which has a span of 33 metres (108 ft) and is 56 metres (184 ft) high. The first chapel on the left as you enter features an early work by Goya, showing St. Bernardino of Siena. Goya included himself in the painting, on the right wearing a yellow jacket. There are also paintings by Zurbarán and Alonso Cano.

CAVA BAJA

Return to the square and exit at the top end along curving **calle Cava Baja**, which

---

San Isidro Labrador

Isidro was a hardworking youth, born in the late 11th century, who toiled in the fields on the far side of the Manzanares river. When he fell asleep on the job, angels apparently descended to plough the field for him. When Vargas, his boss, turned up on a sweltering day, Isidro somehow made a spring of cool water gush forth from the ground. Perhaps most miraculous of all, when Vargas's wife dropped their baby down a well, Isidro made the water rise up, with the baby bobbing on the surface. He was beatified in 1618 and canonised four years later. His feast day is 15 May: a public holiday in Madrid with festivities going on throughout the month.

---

follows the course of the ditch around the 12th- century city wall. Inns sprang up in medieval times to accommodate the merchants and travellers from the stagecoaches and to this day the street is lined with bars and restaurants. The most famous is **Casa Lucio** at No. 35, see ❹, which has been open for more than 40 years. Workshops occupied for centuries by saddlers, coopers and basket makers have now mostly disappeared, replaced by gastrobars, but the street still has a medieval atmosphere.

REAL COLEGIATA DE SAN ISIDRO

Turn right along calle San Bruno, which shortly brings you to calle Toledo and the **Real Colegiata de San Isidro** ❻ (Mon–Sun 7.30am–1pm, 6pm–9pm; guided tours Sat 11.30am; free). This was Madrid's cathedral until the Almudena (see page 42) opened in 1994 and for many Madrilenians is still the most important church.

The Baroque structure was built in 1622 and was originally a Jesuit church. While the original design was by Pedro Sánchez, Francisco Bautista devised the large slate dome and Ventura Rodríguez undertook a neoclassical restoration in the 18th century, when it was renamed after San Isidro, whose remains were brought from the San Andrés church.

Nearby at calle Toledo No. 43, a smell of warm wax exudes from **Victor Ortega** (www.cereriaortega.es; Mon–Fri 9.30am–1.30pm, 5pm–8pm), one

of the last remaining *cererías*, or candle-makers. Their main trade is still in the long white candles for churches, but you can also buy smaller, more decorative ones.

From the church, walk up calle Toledo towards the Plaza Mayor. For lunch in a non-touristy restaurant, try the **Fonda La Lechuga**, see ⑤. Turning right up calle Imperial brings you to the 17th-century **Palacio de Santa Cruz**, the current home to the Ministry of Foreign Affairs. With its slate turrets and spires, it is another of the key buildings of the Habsburg period.

From here, you can stroll back into the Plaza Mayor, down to the Puerta del Sol or along to Plaza de Santa Ana.

Food and Drink

❶ MERCADO DE SAN MIGUEL

Plaza de San Miguel; tel: 91 5424936; www.mercadodesanmiguel.es; Mon–Wed and Sun 10am–midnight, Thurs–Sat 10am–2am; €€

This traditional market is now a gourmet food court that is packed at all hours with locals and tourists, all clutching glasses of wine, vermouth or beer and plates of prawns, oysters, cheese, ham and lots more from the tempting stalls.

❷ CASA PACO

Plaza Puerta Cerrada 11; tel: 91 3663167; www.casapaco1933.es; Tue–Sat 12.30–4pm, 7pm–midnight, Sun 12.30–4pm; €€
Open since the 1930s, Casa Paco is one of the most traditional places for Madrilenian specialities or a cold beer and a tapa at the bar.

❸ JUANA LA LOCA

Puerta de Moros 4; tel 91 364 0525; http://juanalalocamadrid.com; Mon 7pm–

midnight, Tue–Sat 1–5pm, 7pm–midnight, 1am at weekends, Sun 1pm–midnight; €€
With marble tables and white tiled walls, this is a popular spot for a quick bite or a full meal. Order a wedge of tortilla potato omelette, one of the best in Madrid.

❹ CASA LUCIO

Cava Baja 35; tel: 91 3653252; www.casalucio.es; Mon–Sun 1–4pm, 8.30pm–midnight; €€€
This classic Castilian restaurant is a real Madrid institution and attracts a glamorous clientele who come here for the roast meats from the wood-fired oven and the legendary *huevos rotos* – fried eggs on a pile of chips.

❺ FONDA LA LECHUGA

Calle Lechuga 2; tel: 91 3641116; http://fondalalechuga.com; Mon 10.30am–5pm, Tue–Fri 10.30am–5pm, 9pm–midnight, Sat noon–5pm, 9pm–1am; €
The fixed-price lunch in this friendly, family-run restaurant is excellent value with a choice of Spanish specialities that mix the traditional with creative touches.

Changing of the guards at the Palacio Real

ROYAL MADRID

There is a lot to see on this route. As well as the majestic Palacio Real, it takes in two royal convents, the Teatro Real opera house, the splendid Plaza de Oriente square and the Almudena cathedral.

> **DISTANCE:** 5km (3 miles)
> **TIME:** A full day
> **START:** Puerta del Sol
> **END:** Jardines de Sabatini
> **POINTS TO NOTE:** This is an interesting walk even if you do not want to visit all the monuments in one day. If you go to the gardens around the palace at the end, you could combine it with a stroll along the Manzanares river.

In the heart of the main shopping area, we veer off to visit two almost hidden convents founded in the 16th and 17th centuries by the Habsburg monarchs. They look rather unassuming from the outside, but contain astounding collections of artistic treasures.

CALLE ARENAL

From the **Puerta del Sol** ❶, walk along calle Arenal, west from the square. Now a pleasant pedestrianised shopping street, back in medieval times a stream flowed through here, which in the summer would dry out to create a sandy promenade.

On the left at No. 9 is the **Palacio de Gaviria**, where the Marquis of Gaviria, a financier from Seville, used to hold grand parties in the 19th century. Queen Isabella II was a regular guest.

Just beyond it, a wooden shack selling second-hand books stands on the corner of the pasadizo de San Ginés, a lane leading to the **Chocolatería de San Ginés**, see ❶, a Madrid institution that specialises in thick hot chocolate and *churros* – the perfect place to get the energy boost needed for this route.

Back on calle Arenal, next on the left is the **Iglesia de San Ginés** (Mon–Sat 8.45am–1pm, 6pm–9pm, Sun 9.45am–2pm, 6pm–9pm; free), which is now run by the Opus Dei organisation. The church features on the town charter of 1202 but the current structure largely dates from the 19th century. There is an **El Greco** painting in the Santísimo Cristo chapel, but this is not always open to the public.

Artworks in the Monasterio de las Descalzas Reales

MONASTERIO DE LAS DESCALZAS REALES

Turn right off calle Arenal up calle San Martín until you get to the Plaza de la Descalzas. Facing you is the long façade of the **Monasterio de las Descalzas Reales** ❷ (Monastery of the Royal Barefoot Nuns; www.patrimonionacional.es/real-sitio/monasterio-de-las-descalzas-reales; Tue–Sat 10am–2pm, 4–6.30pm, Sun 10am–3pm; guided tour; free Wed–Thu 4–6.30pm for EU citizens). The convent, where there is still a small community of nuns of the Franciscan order of the Poor Clares, may look rather austere but inside is a secret world that gives a fascinating insight into the Habsburg royal family.

Originally a palace, it was turned into a convent in the mid-16th century by Juana, King Felipe II's sister. The daughters of other royal and aristocratic families joined the order and a lot of rather valuable donations followed over the years, capturing the richness of Spain's Golden Age. Some of these are now in the Prado museum, but you can still see Flemish tapestries, frescoes and a great many royal portraits. There are also paintings by El Greco, Titian, Rubens, Velázquez and Zurbarán as well as sculptures by Pedro de Mena and Pompeo de Leoni. From the upper cloister, peep into the inner courtyard where the nuns grow their own vegetables.

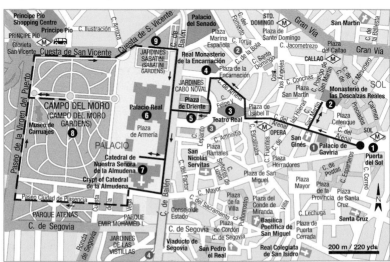

PLAZA DE ISABEL II

Return to calle Arenal and continue west until you reach the **Plaza de Isabel II**, originally a space just outside the medieval city wall where several streams used to merge. Washtubs and bathhouses were set up to take advantage of the water supply, while sandbanks served as a makeshift stage where performances used to take place until a theatre was built in the 18th century, which was replaced the following century by the Teatro Real opera house.

TEATRO REAL

Madrid's grand opera house, the **Teatro Real** ❸ (Royal Theatre; www.teatroreal.com; guided tours 10.30am–1pm), stages its own prestigious productions and hosts operas from around the world, as well as being used for concerts and dance performances. You usually need to book online well ahead to get tickets but the theatre's current success belies its rather rocky history.

Construction began in 1818, but the first performance did not take place until 1850 as the gigantic theatre was plagued by a plethora of structural problems, caused mainly by the fact that it was built over an underground lake, but also because of a lack of funds. Following damage during the Civil War and several periods of closure, it reopened in 1997 after lavish refurbishment as a state-of-the-art venue with one of the largest stages in the world.

REAL MONASTERIO DE LA ENCARNACIÓN

Walk up calle Arrieta, along the north side of the opera house, to the tranquil Plaza de la Encarnación. The **Real Monasterio de la Encarnación** ❹ (Royal Monastery of the Incarnation; www.patrimonionacional.es/real-sitio/real-monasterio-de-la-encarnacion; Tue–Sat 10am–2pm, 4–6.30pm, Sun 10am–3pm; guided tour; free Wed–Thu 4–6.30pm for EU citizens) was founded in 1611 by Queen Margarita de Austria, the wife of King Felipe III, and is still home to a few Augustinian nuns.

Designed by Juan Gómez de Mora and Fray Alberto de la Madre de Dios, it is a graceful structure that contains paintings by leading artists including Vicente Carducho and José de Ribera, many painted especially for the convent. The elegant church was restored in the mid-18th century by Ventura Rodríguez, who added marble from various regions of Spain.

It is worth visiting just to see the extraordinary reliquary room, with a coffered ceiling, which is filled with some 1,500 relics in glass and mahogony cases. The most intriguing exhibit is a vial containing what is purported to be the blood of Pantaleon, the doctor saint, which mysteriously liquefies and turns bright red on his feast day, 27 July. Madrilenians queue around the block to see the miracle for themselves and only in years of great crisis does the phenomenon fail to occur.

The stately Plaza de Oriente and the Teatro Real

PLAZA DE ORIENTE

On leaving the convent, walk through the gardens opposite, which are part of the vast **Plaza de Oriente** ❺. Or if it is lunchtime, one of Madrid's most traditional restaurants, **La Bola**, see ❷, is nearby.

The semicircular space, landscaped with flowerbeds and shaded by trees, was initially laid out during the reign of Napoleon's brother, Joseph Bonaparte, who was king of Spain from 1808 to 1813 during the French occupation. Construction was still underway in the mid-19th century, when the bronze equestrian statue of **Felipe IV** was installed. Designed by Pedro Tacca and based on a painting by Velázquez, the statue was made in 1639 with the help of the Italian scientist Galileo Galilei, who solved the difficulties presented by a horse rearing up on its back legs by making it hollow in front and solid at the back to prevent it from toppling over.

The other statues in the square – of Roman emperors born in Spain, Visigoth leaders and Christian monarchs – were made to adorn the parapet of the palace but never made it up there. The official reason was that the building could not support their weight or they might fall off. It is also claimed, however, that Isabel de Farnese, Felipe V's second wife, refused to allow their elevation after she had a nightmare in which they crashed down on top of her.

The French influence is reinforced by the lead mansard roofs, stuccoed façades and wrought-iron balconies of the elegant buildings flanking the square – all a reflection of the opulence of the early 20th century. The stylish **Café de Oriente**, see ❸, on the ground floor of one of these buildings, is a comfortable place to rest your feet.

PALACIO REAL

You might be wondering why the square is called *Oriente*, as this is the western edge of the city, but the name actually refers to the eastern side of the massive **Palacio Real** ❻ (Royal Palace; www.patrimonionacional.es/real-sitio/palacio-real-de-madrid; Oct–Mar

Churros & chocolate

Whether for breakfast, in the late afternoon, at the end of a night out or at a street festival, Madrilenians love dipping sugary *churro* fritters into a cup of dense hot chocolate. This is an experience you should definitely try while in the city. Made from just flour, water and salt, *churros* are ridged strips of batter that are piped into huge vats of bubbling oil and fried until golden brown. The strips are then snipped into short lengths with the ends sometimes pressed together to form a loop. Churros must always be consumed as soon as possible as they go stodgy very quickly. The hot chocolate is more like a sauce than a drink and is made from slabs of bitter chocolate melted with cornflour, sugar and milk. Naughty but very nice indeed.

The lavish dining room in the Palacio Real

10am–6pm, Apr–Sept 10am–8pm; free last two hours for EU citizens), standing on the other side of the space.

The Palacio Real is used only for official ceremonies and events (when it is closed to the public) – the state dining room can seat 145 people and is lit by 25 chandeliers. The Spanish monarchs, King Felipe VI and Queen Letizia, favour a more low-key profile and their main residence is the less ostentatious Palacio de la Zarzuela just outside the centre.

The palace stands on the site of the Alcázar, the fortress built by the Moors in the ninth century on a ridge above the Manzanares river. The strategic location, with panoramic views across the countryside, was ideal for watching out for approaching enemies.

When the Alcázar, originally built of wood, burned down on Christmas Eve 1734, it gave King Felipe V the opportunity to replace it with a magnificent stone and granite structure along French-Italian lines. The original architect, Felipe Juvarra, planned a building twice the size, but he died in 1739 and his student Giovanni Battista Sacchetti took over and modified the project. The first king to live there was Carlos III in 1764 and the last was Alfonso XIII, who left when he abdicated the throne in 1931.

Be prepared for a visual onslaught inside, as the ornate decoration bombards your senses at every turn. The endless lavish rooms include the **throne room**, where Tiepolo painted the ceiling with an allegory of the Majesty of Spain.

The **Gasparini room**, with embroidered silver silk covering the walls and a swirling marble mosaic floor, was restored in the 1990s but has otherwise remained practically unchanged since the time when Carlos III used to get dressed here in the presence of his court.

The **Museo de las Colecciones Reales** (Museum of the Royal Collections) has been built on the hillside below the palace and is scheduled to open by 2020. The large structure will display part of the extensive royal art holdings and hold temporary exhibitions.

CATEDRAL DE NUESTRA SEÑORA DE LA ALMUDENA

Facing the palace entrance, on the opposite side of the square, is the 19th-century **Catedral de Nuestra Señora de la Almudena** ❼ (www.catedraldela almudena.es; Mon–Sun 9am–8.30pm; July–Aug 10am–9pm; free). Begun in the 19th century but not finished until 1993, Madrid's cathedral combines quite a variety of architectural styles, with the neo-Gothic interior contained within a neoclassical shell, devised by Fernando Chueca Goitia and Carlos Sidro in the 1940s. Inside, light streams in through rose windows and the dome crowns the Latin-cross transept.

Be sure to visit the **crypt** (Mon–Sun 10am–9pm; entrance on calle Cuesta de la Vega) to see the neo-Romanesque capitals, stained-glass windows and the figure of the Virgin of the Almudena.

Cross the road when you come out of the crypt to see vestiges of the walls built by Moors in the 9th century and Christians in the 12th century; they now form part of the **Parque Emir Mohammed I**, which is sometimes used for concerts.

THE PALACE GARDENS

If you still have energy left at this point, you can stroll around the palace gardens. Continue down the hill through the Parque de Atenas, then turn right along the Paseo de la Vírgen del Puerto to the entrance of the **Campo del Moro ❽** gardens below the palace. For centuries the steep escarpment was an effective natural defence, but the landscaping of the hillside created gently sloping lawns.

Turn right when you come out, then skirt the gardens by turning right again up the Cuesta de San Vicente until you come to the entrance to the **Sabatini ❾** gardens on the north side of the palace.

If you don't fancy such a trek when you come out of the crypt, cross the viaduct over the calle Segovia to get to the shady **El Ventorillo** terrace, see ❹ – usually called Las Vistillas – where you can sit and enjoy a refreshing drink.

Food and Drink

❶ CHOCOLATERÍA SAN GINÉS

Pasadizo de San Ginés 5;
tel: 91 3656546; https://chocolateria
sangines.com; Mon–Sun 24 hours; €
In business since 1894, this is the most well-known place to indulge in churros with hot chocolate. You might have to queue at busy times but service is brisk.

❷ LA BOLA

Calle La Bola 5; tel: 91 547 6930;
http://en.labola.es; Mon–Sat 1.30–5pm,
Sun 1.30–5pm; €€
Pretty restaurant with a red frontage founded in 1870 that specialises in traditional Madrilenian dishes, particularly *cocido madrileño* stew, which is served in earthenware pots. Book ahead.

❸ CAFÉ DE ORIENTE

Plaza de Oriente 2; tel: 91 5471564;
www.cafedeoriente.es; Mon–Sun 8.30am–
1.30am, Fri–Sat until 2.30am; €€
A smart café-restaurant with a terrace on the square, this is a good option for everything from breakfast to cocktails. The restaurant serves traditional dishes such as braised beef cheeks in red wine; the café has tapas and burgers.

❹ EL VENTORRILLO

Calle Bailén 14, Las Vistillas; tel: 91 366 3578; Mar–Sept Mon–Sat 11am–1am, Sun 11am–midnight; €€
One of Madrid's best-loved terraces, this is one of the most romantic spots in the city. While you might sit down planning to have just a coffee or a beer, don't be surprised if you are still there hours later, ordering a plate of prawns and a watching the sun go down.

Strolling down the Paseo del Prado's shady boulevard

THE PASEO DEL PRADO

This walk explores the top half of the Paseo del Prado and the elegant streets of the Jerónimos district, taking in the impressive Museo Nacional Thyssen–Bornemisza.

DISTANCE: 1.5km (1 mile)
TIME: Half a day
START: Plaza de Cibeles
END: Plaza de Neptuno
POINTS TO NOTE: Although the route is short, visiting the museums takes time so do bear that in mind. Afterwards, you could go to the Retiro Park (route 6) or the Barrio de Las Letras (route 7).

Madrid's major museums are situated along the Paseo del Prado, also known as the Paseo del Arte – the Art Walk. The lower section, where the Prado and Reina Sofía museums are situated, is explored separately in route 5, as it can be exhausting and overwhelming to visit them all on the same day.

PLAZA DE CIBELES

Traffic streams at all hours of the day and night around the **Plaza de Cibeles ❶**, which connects the key parts of the city. In the centre of the square, the

Fuente de Cibeles is one of Madrid's main landmarks. The fountain features Cybele, the goddess of nature, in a chariot pulled by two lions. A symbol of the fertility of the land around the city, the fountain is where fans of Real Madrid football club converge after important victories.

Occupying a huge block on the corner of calle de Alcalá and the Paseo del Prado is the **Banco de España** (Bank of Spain), with a magnificent entrance decorated with sculptures by Jerónimo Suñol. Across calle de Alcalá, on the northwest corner, is the **Palacio de Buenavista**, built for the Duchess of Alba in the 18th century and now the headquarters of the Spanish army.

The neo-Baroque **Palacio de Linares** takes up the northeast corner. Built in the late 19th century for the Marquis of Linares, the palace has sumptuous interiors and is said to be haunted (guided tours Sat–Sun 11am, noon, 1pm). Also in the building is the **Casa de América** (www.casaamerica.es; Mon–Fri 11am–7.30pm, Sat 11am–3pm; free), a Latin American cultural

The Fuente de Cibeles and the Palacio de Comunicaciones

centre with a lively programme of exhibitions, concerts and talks.

Palacio de Comunicaciones

Dominating the square is the curving white **Palacio de Comunicaciones**, the gloriously ornate former main post office designed by Antonio Palacios, the man behind several of Madrid's grandest buildings of the early 20th century. It is now the City Hall and also houses **Centro Centro** (http://centrocentro.org; Tue–Sun 10am–8pm; free), where there are usually a few exhibitions on. It is worth going in just to see the elaborate interior. Zoom up to the observation deck (Tue–Sun 10.30am–1.30pm, 4pm–7pm) for panoramic views across the city – or just have a drink in the chic terrace **bar**, see ❶, on the sixth floor (open from 1pm).

PASEO DEL PRADO

The Plaza de Cibeles marks the start of the **Paseo del Prado**, laid out during the Enlightenment period in the 18th century. The northern section of the boulevard, down to Plaza de Neptuno, was devoted to leisure – a place to walk and parade around in carriages – while the lower half (see route 5) was more about education, science and medicine.

On the left at No. 5, it is easy to miss the **Museo Naval** (Naval Museum; www.armada.mde.es/museonaval; Tue–Sun 10am–7pm), where highlights include a map drawn up in 1500 by Juan de la Cosa, which was the first to show the territories of the New World. Walk up calle Montalbán to see the main part of the building, the **Cuartel General de la Armada**, the headquarters of the Spanish Navy Ministry, with an elaborate façade featuring Portuguese Manueline decoration.

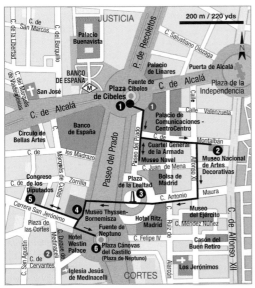

Lichtenstein at the Thyssen-Bornemisza

MUSEO NACIONAL DE ARTES DECORATIVAS

At the top of calle Montalbán at No. 12 is the **Museo Nacional de Artes Decorativas ❷** (National Museum of Decorative Arts; http://mnartesdecorativas. mcu.es; Tue–Sat 9.30am–3pm, Thu also 5pm–8pm, Sun 10am–30m), housed in a grand 19th-century palace. The excellent displays include tapestries, leatherwork, ceramics, jewellery, fans and furniture, as well as an 18th-century Valencian kitchen with elaborate tiled walls.

Turn left out of the museum, then left again along the tree-lined calle Alfonso XI and take the second right down the broad calle Antonio Maura. This is the elegant Jerónimos area, with red-brick apartment buildings with wrought-iron mirador balconies. You might recognise the streets from Pedro Almodóvar's film *Women on the Verge of a Nervous Breakdown*.

PLAZA DE LA LEALTAD

Calle Antonio Maura leads down to the **Plaza de la Lealtad ❸**, where an obelisk marks the centre of the **Monumento a los Caídos por España**, a cenotaph built in tribute to those who died in Madrid's battle against French troops on 2 May 1808. It now also honours all those who have given their lives for Spain.

On the right of the square is the **Bolsa de Comercio** (www.bolsamadrid.es; visits by appointment only). Built in the late 19th century, Madrid's stock exchange has a concave, arcaded façade that makes the triangular site look much bigger than it actually is.

On the opposite side of the square is the **Hotel Ritz** (see page 94), built in 1908 by the French architect Charles Mewes, who had previously designed the Ritz hotels in Paris and London.

MUSEO NACIONAL THYSSEN-BORNEMISZA

Cross the Paseo del Prado to reach the **Museo Nacional Thyssen-Bornemisza ❹** (museothyssen.org; tel: 91 7911370; Mon noon–4pm, permanent collections only; Tue–Sun 10am–7pm; free Mon). The museum's superlative displays of Western art from the 13th to the 20th centuries were built up by Baron Heinrich Thyssen-Bornemisza and extended by his son, Hans Heinrich, who died in 2002. Considered to be one of the best collections in the world, around 1,000 artworks are on show in the Palacio de Villahermosa, a handsome neoclassical structure that was remodelled to house the museum by Rafael Moneo.

Visiting the Thyssen-Bornemisza

Divided into Old Masters and New Masters, the displays are arranged over three floors, in chronological order, starting at the top of the building. The baron's widow, Carmen Thyssen-Bornemisza, has overseen the museum since his death and her own prestigious collection is displayed in a wing added in 2004,

Under the Hotel Westin dome   *Franz Marc's The Dream (1912) at the Thyssen–Bornemisza*

with paintings by Gauguin, Van Gogh, Braque and Picasso.

On the second floor, **Level 2**, masterpieces include Domenico Ghirlandaio's *Portrait of Goivanna Tornabuoni* (1488), Hans Holbein the Younger's *Portrait of Henry VIII* and *Jesus among the Doctors* by Albrecht Dürer.

On **Level 1**, highlights include *Woman with a Parasol* by Pierre-Auguste Renoir, *Swaying Dancer* by Edgar Degas, *Metropolis* by George Grosz, *Seated Woman* by Juan Gris and *Hotel Room* by Edward Hopper. The displays continue on **Level 0**, the ground floor, with works by Salvador Dalí and Roy Lichtenstein.

CONGRESO DE LOS DIPUTADOS

Turn right out of the museum and right again up Carrera de San Jerónimo. On the right is the **Congreso de los Diputados** ❺ (tel: 91 390 6525; www.congreso.es; guided tours Mon noon without reservation, Fri noon and Sat 10.30am–12.30pm with prior telephone or online reservation). More commonly known as **Las Cortes**, the seat of the Spanish Parliament (1842–50) has a neoclassical portico guarded by lions, which were cast using bronze from cannons seized during the African war of 1860.

Opposite is the triangular **Plaza de las Cortes**, with a statue of Miguel de Cervantes marking the entrance to the Barrio de Las Letras (see route 7). On the southwest corner of the square is the Parisian-style **Hotel Westin Palace** (see page 94), which opened in 1912

and has always been a favourite haunt of artists and writers, including Dalí and Picasso. You can enjoy a drink under the stained-glass dome in the sumptuous Rotonda lounge, or for a beer and a tapa in a more down to earth setting, head for **Taberna El Rincón de José**, see ❷, around the corner.

Marking the end of this part of the Paseo del Prado is the **Plaza de Neptuno** ❻. The marble **Fuente de Neptuno** in the centre features Neptune, god of the sea, holding a trident and standing on a shell-shaped chariot drawn by seahorses.

Food and Drink

❶ BAR TERRAZA, CENTRO CENTRO

Plaza de Cibeles 1; tel 91 480 0008; centrocentro.org; Sun–Thur 1pm–2am, Fri-Sat 1pm–2.30am; €
Enjoy the views across the city with a coffee or a cocktail from this chic outdoor bar on the sixth floor of the Centro Centro cultural centre, where there is often a DJ later in the evening.

❷ TABERNA EL RINCÓN DE JOSÉ

Calle Duque de Medinaceli 12; tel: 91 429 9073; Mon–Sat 9am–2am, Sun noon–4pm; €€
Charming bar with Spanish and Basque food that is good for tapas, lunch or just a quick drink. Order a plate of ham and the tomato and tuna salad. The steak, served in slices, is good for sharing with a glass of Rioja.

The Museo del Prado, fronted by a statue of Diego Velázquez

THE PRADO AND REINA SOFÍA MUSEUMS

Many people go to Madrid just to visit the Prado, but there is a lot more to see on the Paseo del Prado, however, with contemporary art at the Reina Sofía and CaixaForum museums and the tranquil Royal Botanic Garden for relaxing in between.

DISTANCE: 1km (0.6 mile)
TIME: A full day
START: Museo del Prado
END: Museo Nacional de Arte Contemporáneo Reina Sofía
POINTS TO NOTE: The overall distance covered will of course depend on how many museums you visit. You could combine it with routes 6 or 7.

This stretch of the Paseo del Prado more than lives up to its alternative name as the Paseo del Arte (Art Walk). Allow as much time as possible to enjoy not only visiting the museums but also taking in the spirit of the boulevard itself, which was created to improve the quality of life of the Madrilenians.

THE MUSEO DEL PRADO

The **Museo del Prado** ❶ (Prado Museum; tel: 902 107077; www.museodelprado.es; Mon–Sat 10am–8pm, Sun 10am–7pm; free last two hours) is one of the greatest museums in the world

and you could spend days – or indeed a lifetime – contemplating the astounding displays in its many rooms. As well as superb works by Spanish masters such as El Greco, Velázquez, and Goya, there are wonderful Italian and Flemish collections with paintings by Raphael, Titian, Tintoretto, Bosch and Rubens. There are usually two or three temporary exhibitions running as well.

Designed by Juan de Villanueva in 1785, the neoclassical building was originally intended to be a natural history museum, part of Carlos III's grand plan for the Paseo del Prado as a place of learning and leisure. It was not until the reign of Fernando VII (1814–33) that it was decided to use the building to house the royal collections of art, with the museum opening in 1819.

At the beginning of the 21st century, Pritzker prize-winning architect Rafael Moneo designed a new section linking the main structure to the cloister of the Jerónimos church behind the building. Used for temporary exhibitions, it features sculptural doors by Cristina Iglesias.

Admiring the masterpieces in the Museo del Prado

The Prado's collections were commissioned and acquired by Spain's monarchs over the centuries and reflect their links with other countries as well as their personal tastes. The museum also received substantial holdings following the disentailment of religious property in the 19th century. Although the museum is vast, the Prado only displays about 10 percent of its collections.

Visiting the Prado

Most visitors only have a few hours to spend in the museum so it is advisable to decide what you most want to see. You might want to concentrate on the Velázquez, Goya and Bosch paintings. That said, even the best of intentions are likely to go astray as you stroll through the halls, given the quality and quantity of work on display, and just wandering around making your own discoveries has a lot to be said for it too.

Access to the museum is at the north end of the building – the Goya entrance. You usually have to queue to buy tickets, so if possible, save time by pre-booking online. Pick up a floorplan when you go in; it highlights 50 of the key works in the museum.

Spanish collections

The Prado's unsurpassable Spanish paintings begin with Romanesque art and end with Goya. Masterpieces from the 12th to the 16th centuries include works by Bartolomé Bermejo, Juan de Juanes and Pedro Berruguete. The 17th-century displays are particularly impressive, with paintings by José de Ribera, Murillo and Zurbarán.

The Triumph of Bacchus (1628–29), by Velázquez

El Greco

Domenikos Theotokopoulos (1541–1614), known as El Greco (The Greek), was born in Crete and lived in Toledo from 1577 until his death, working on his dramatic canvases that feature ethereal elongated figures in hues of grey, mauve and yellow. *The Nobleman with his Hand on his Chest*, restored in the 1990s, is one of the earliest he painted in Spain. One of his last works was The *Adoration of the Shepherds*, which he painted for his own burial chapel.

Velázquez

The paintings by Diego de Velázquez (1599–1660) are in the centre of the first floor. *Las Meninas* (*The Maids of Honour* or *The Family of Philip IV*), which many experts consider to be the greatest work of Western art, is in the oval room at the heart of the museum. Painted in 1656, this is the work that attracts the greatest crowds. Everyone is captivated and fascinated by this puzzle of a picture, in which Velázquez portrayed himself, perhaps painting the king and queen, who are reflected in a mirror, watched by their daughter the Infanta Margarita, her maids of honour and other court figures. The role of each character in the painting and what they represent has intrigued both art historians and the casual viewer for centuries. Try and look at it from different angles, from close up and at a distance.

The Surrender of Breda depicts the triumph of the Spanish over the Dutch at the Siege of Breda in 1625, with the victor humbly accepting the key to the town. In *The Triumph of Bacchus* (better known as *The Topers or The Drunkards*) and the later work *The Spinners* (also known as *The Fable of Arachne*), he painted mythological figures as everyday characters.

Goya

The Goya works are at the southern end of the museum on the ground, first and second floors. Francisco de Goya (1746–1828) was court artist to Carlos IV and painted numerous royal portraits. In *Carlos IV and his Family* (1800), he pays tribute to Velázquez by painting himself in the left-hand corner; the king has an absentminded look and the queen has beady eyes. Two of his most powerful paintings, *The Second of May, 1808, in Madrid: the Charge of the Mamelukes*, and *The Third of May, 1808, in Madrid: The Executions at Príncipe Pío*, commemorate the Madrilenians desperate and unsuccessful attempts to prevent their city falling under French control.

Goya's nightmarish *Black Paintings* were created at the end of his life, originally painted on the walls of his house by the Manzanares river. For a lighter mood, go up to the second floor to see the cartoons he painted for the Royal Tapestry Factory (see page 57), depicting typical scenes and local festivals.

Flemish, German and Dutch collections

The rich collections include Rogier van der Weyden's great masterpiece, *Descent from the Cross*, which Felipe II

The much-admired Garden of Earthly Delights, by Bosch

inherited from his aunt, Mary of Hungary, and Self-Portrait at 26 by Albrecht Dürer (1471–1528).

King Felipe II was fascinated by the work of Hieronymous Bosch (1450–1516) and had several of his best works at his monastery-palace at El Escorial (see page 82). *The Haywain* is inspired by the Flemish proverb: "The world is a haywain from which every man takes what he can." His most famous creation, *The Garden of Earthly Delights* (c. 1505) shows mankind engaged in ephemeral pleasures in the central panel, with Paradise on the left and Hell on the right.

Only a handful of the Prado's extensive holdings of paintings by Peter Paul Rubens (1577–1640) are on display, but these include *The Adoration of the Magi* and *The Three Graces* (circa 1635), which features the faces of both the artist's wives.

Italian collections

Among the superlative early Italian works, which came mainly from the royal collections, are *The Story of Nastagio degli Onesti* panels by Sandro Botticelli (1445–1510) and the delicate *Annunciation* by Fra Angelico (circa 1400–55).

The identity of the sitter in the magnificent *Portrait of a Cardinal* (1510) by Raphael (1483-1520) has never been discovered. Titian, who worked for both Carlos V and Felipe II, painted *The Emperor Charles V in Mühlberg* following the battle in 1547 when the emperor triumphed over the Protestants. Among the paintings by Tintoretto (1518–94) is *Christ Washing the Disciples' Feet*, which is a superb example of his extraordinary skill at perspective.

You probably need a break when you emerge from the Prado. The museum has a pleasant terrace café by the exit, or you could walk up the steps on the right, which lead to calle Ruiz de Alarcón, and turn right along the street to the **Murillo Café**, see ❶, at No. 27.

When you have recovered, turn left out of the café and immediately right into the **Plaza de Murillo**, at the southern end of the Prado building, where there are fountains of children playing with dolphins, designed by Ventura Rodríguez in 1781.

REAL JARDÍN BOTÁNICO

On the left of the square is the peaceful **Real Jardín Botánico** ❷ (Royal Botanic Garden; www.rjb.csic.es; Mon–Sun 10am–dusk), a great oasis in which to spend a quiet hour between museums, strolling among plants from all over the world.

At the entrance, look at the neoclassical gate, the Puerta de Murillo, designed by Juan de Villanueva. Founded in the 18th century, the garden was originally devised by the botanist Casimiro Gómez Ortega to cultivate the plants brought back from Spanish colonies all around the world. Back then, the Reina Sofía museum just down the road was a hospital, so the idea was to provide a supply of plants for medicinal purposes.

The vertical garden at CaixaForum

Old varieties of rose flank the Paseo de Carlos III, which leads down to the Puerta Real, a gate designed by Sabatini. On the second level, look out for the elm tree known as *Pantalones*, because the trunk is divided into two and it looks like a pair of trousers. There is an oval pond on the upper level, surrounded by trees including a Canarian palm. The pavilion at the back was originally a hothouse but is now used for temporary exhibitions.

Cross the Paseo del Prado. If you are ready for lunch, there are lots of good places around the Plaza Platería Martínez, such as **Vinoteca Moratín**, see ❷.

CAIXAFORUM

Continuing down the Paseo del Prado, on the right at No. 36 you reach the **CaixaForum** cultural centre ❸ (https:// obrasociallacaixa.org/es/cultura/caixa forum-madrid; Mon–Sun 10am–8pm). The building, originally an electrical power plant dating back to the beginning of the 20th century, was remodelled in 2008 by the Swiss architects Herzog & de Meuron, who added a galvanised steel outer casing and a vertical garden. Inside, the seven floors are linked by a dramatic white concrete staircase. As well as temporary exhibitions, there is a varied programme of concerts, talks and other activities.

Walk down the last block of the Paseo del Prado to reach the Glorieta de Atocha crossroads, with Atocha train station on the left, and cross over calle Atocha to the Reina Sofía museum on Plaza de Santa Isabel.

MUSEO NACIONAL CENTRO DE ARTE REINA SOFÍA

The **Museo Nacional Centro de Arte Reina Sofía** ❹ (Reina Sofía National Museum Art Centre; calle Santa Isabel 52; tel: 91 774 1000; www.museoreina sofia.es; Mon and Wed–Sat 10am–9pm, Sun 10am–7pm; free last two hours, Sun from 2.30pm) is Madrid's enormous museum of contemporary art, where there are usually three or four major temporary exhibitions underway, as well as the extensive displays of selections of the permanent collection.

Pablo Picasso's great masterpiece *Guernica* draws the biggest crowds but there is a lot more to see, including superlative works by Salvador Dalí, Joan Miró and Antoni Tàpies. International artists include Georges Braque, Julian Schnabel and Richard Serra. The museum is housed in the 18th-century Hospital General de San Carlos, with a new section designed by French architect Jean Nouvel.

Visiting the Reina Sofía

It is easy to spend all day in this museum, navigating the four floors of the main building –accessed via glass lifts on the outside of the structure – plus the galleries in the new wing. Luckily, there are two great places to eat, drink and rest: **Arzábal** ❸ and **NuBel** ❹, both with outdoor tables, as well as a good shop for books and gifts.

CaixaForum's staircase   *Lichtenstein outside the Reina Sofía Museum*

The work is displayed chronologically, starting on Level 2, which covers 1900–45. Artists represented include Julio González, Joan Miró, Juan Gris and Georges Braque. Among the paintings by Salvador Dalí are *Girl at the Window* and *Face of the Great Masturbator*.

Guernica

Pablo Picasso (1881–1973) painted his masterpiece for the Spanish Pavilion of the 1937 Paris World Fair, in response to the bombing earlier that year of the town of Guernica in the Basque Country by German planes on the orders of General Franco. The painting has come to symbolise universal suffering and the savagery of war. Although most people are familiar with the image, the emotional impact of seeing the original is often overwhelming.

The displays continue on Level 3, spanning the period 1945–68, with works by Antoni Tàpies, Eduardo Chillida, Antonio López and Antonio Saura. Level 4 is used for temporary exhibitions and the permanent collections continue on Level 1, the ground floor, where highlights from 1962 to 1982 include sculptures by Richard Serra and Juan Muñoz.

Food and Drink

❶ MURILLO CAFÉ

Calle Ruiz de Alarcón 27; tel: 91 3693689; www.murillocafe.com; Mon–Sat 9.30am–11pm, Sun noon–6pm; €€
An attractive café with terrace tables, where you can stop for breakfast, coffee, brunch or lunch. There is a range of fresh juices, salads and tasty pizzas.

❷ VINOTECA MORATÍN

Calle Moratín 36; tel: 91 1276085; www.vinotecamoratin.com; Tue–Sat 1–4pm, 7pm–midnight; €€
Modern Spanish food with a seasonal menu and excellent Spanish and international wines in a relaxed bistro setting. One of the best places in the area for lunch or dinner, with reasonable prices too.

❸ ARZÁBAL

Museo Reina Sofía; tel: 91 5286828; www.arzabal.com; Mon–Sun 9am–1.30am; €€
Try contemporary Spanish tapas and full meals from chef Iván Morales, or just have a drink as there are bar and restaurant areas with indoor and outdoor tables. The terrace is lovely for a romantic dinner. If you are not in the museum, there is also access from the street on Ronda de Atocha.

❹ NUBEL

Museo Reina Sofía; tel: 91 5301761; www.nubel.es; Mon–Wed 9.30am–1am, Thu 9.30am–2am, Fri-Sat 9.30am–2.30am; €€
Everything from breakfast to burgers, coffee to cocktails is available in this futuristic space in the Nouvel wing of the Reina Sofía museum, which will thrill fans of contemporary design.

Monument to Alfonso XII and the boating lake

THE RETIRO PARK AND ATOCHA

The Madrilenians are fond of their main park, particularly on Sunday mornings, when families come to stroll around and sit at the many outdoor cafés. It is well worth exploring the area to the south too, where there a few lesser-known sights.

DISTANCE: 4km (2.5 miles)
TIME: Three hours
START: Puerta de Alcalá
END: Real Fábrica de Tápices
POINTS TO NOTE: This is a good walk to do after a morning at one of the major museums. The route is intended to give you an idea of the layout of the Retiro park, rather than to be followed to the letter.

There is always a lot going on in the Retiro, where people come to jog, row boats, do yoga, play guitar, visit exhibitions or just read a book at a café terrace. South of the park is Atocha train station, with the fascinating Real Fábrica de Tapices (Royal Tapestry Factory) nearby.

PUERTA DE ALCALÁ

Dominating the circular Plaza de la Independencia, by the main entrance to the park, is the **Puerta de Alcalá** ❶ (Alcalá Gate), a triumphal arch built for Carlos III by Francesco Sabatini in the late 18th century. The neoclassical granite structure is one of Madrid's most important symbols.

For a quick breakfast or snack, or to buy sandwiches for a picnic, pop into **Rodilla**, see ❶, before going into the park.

PARQUE DEL BUEN RETIRO

The northeast corner of the Plaza de la Independencia leads to the **Parque del Buen Retiro** (Retiro Park; Mon–Sun Oct–Mar 9am–10pm, Apr–Sept 9am–midnight).

The rectangular park has evolved from its origins in the 17th century as the gardens of the Palacio del Buen Retiro, which had been built for Felipe IV. This was a huge complex on the hill behind the Prado, but only the ballroom and one wing have survived. The Retiro became a public park in 1868.

From the entrance, Avenida Méjico leads up diagonally to the lake, one of the few surviving elements from the old palace. Back in the 17th century, it was used for extravagant theatrical performances. Now it's only rowing boats caus-

Fountain in Retiro Park

Music in the park

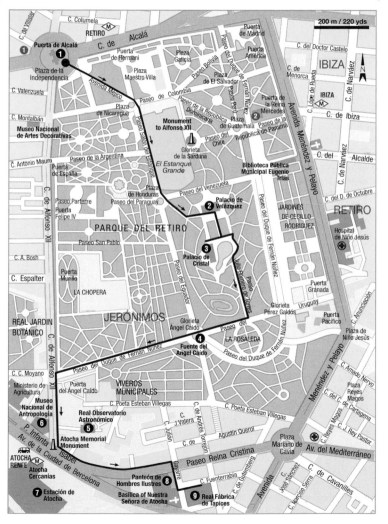

The exquisite Palacio de Cristal

ing ripples in the water (available for hire 10am–sunset). Presiding over it is the semicircular **Monumento a Alfonso XII**, designed by José Grases Riera in 1922.

Turn right and walk along the promenade flanking the lake. At the end, bear diagonally left to reach the **Palacio de Velázquez ❷**, a large pavilion built in the late 19th century now used for exhibitions staged by the Reina Sofía museum (see page 52). Adjacent, overlooking a smaller lake, the **Palacio de Cristal ❸**, was built around the same time and is also now an exhibition venue. A superb

example of iron and glass architecture, it was inspired by London's Crystal Palace and the Palm House at Kew Gardens.

Continuing south, you reach the broad Paseo de Uruguay. Opposite is the **Rosaleda**, a semicircular rose garden. Perhaps the most intriguing of the many fountains in the park is the **Fuente del Ángel Caído ❹** (Fallen Angel Fountain), standing where the Paseo de Uruguay meets the Paseo de Cuba. Made by Ricardo Bellver in 1878, it represents Lucifer's descent to Hell and is one of the few statues in the world that celebrate the devil.

There are lots of cafés dotted around the park, but the most attractive is **Florida Retiro**, see ❷, a pavilion on the eastern edge behind the lake.

To explore beyond the park, from the Ángel Caído fountain, continue down the Paseo del Fernán Nuñez to the exit on calle Alfonso XII.

Turning left out of the park, immediately on the left is the **Real Observatorio Astronómico ❺** (Royal Astronomic Observatory; www.ign.es/rom/visitas/reservas.html; Fri 4.30pm, Sat noon–4.30pm, Sun noon; guided tours in Spanish only, advance reservation required). You must book ahead to visit the observatory, a superb neoclassical structure designed by Juan de Villanueva.

Continuing down calle Alfonso XII, the grandiose building with ceramic decoration on the right is the **Ministerio de Agricultura** (Ministry of Agriculture), built at the end of the 19th century.

Visiting the bullring

You can visit Madrid's bullring and its museum without actually seeing a bullfight. Leave the Retiro park on the Plaza de la Independencia and jump on the metro straight to Ventas station, emerging at the **Plaza de Toros de Las Ventas** (Las Ventas Bullring; www.las-ventas.com). The arena, inaugurated in 1934, is the biggest in Spain with a diameter of 60 metres (197 ft) and room for 24,000 spectators. The **Museo Taurino** (Bullfighting Museum; http://lasventastour.com; Mon–Sun 10am–5.30pm, 1.30pm on bullfight days) provides a good overview of what bullfighting is all about with a tour taking in the Mexican-style chapel where the bullfighters pray before the fight, the surgery and the suits of lights worn by famous matadors, along with their capes and swords.

The luxuriant Estación de Atocha

MUSEO NACIONAL DE ANTROPOLOGÍA

The neoclassical structure at the bottom of the hill on the right is the **Museo Nacional de Antropología** ❻ (National Museum of Anthropology; www.mecd.gob.es/mnantropologia; Tue–Sat 9.30am–8pm, Sun 10am–3pm; free Sat after 2pm and Sun), with Tuareg and Berber exhibits from North Africa and mummies of Guanches, the original inhabitants of the Canary Islands.

AROUND ATOCHA

Opposite is the **Estación de Atocha** ❼ (Atocha Station). The 1992 circular red-brick entrance designed by Rafael Moneo adjoins the old ironwork station, which has been turned into a hothouse of palm trees.

Walk east along the Paseo de la Infanta Isabel to the corner of calle Julián Gayarre. The belltower belongs to the **Panteón de Hombres Ilustres** ❽ (Pantheon of Illustrious Men; Tue–Sat 10am–2pm, 4–6.30pm, Sun 10am–3pm; free), home to elaborate tombs of leading politicians of the 19th century. The pantheon occupies the cloister of the neo-Baroque **Basílica de Nuestra Señora de Atocha** (Basilica of Our Lady of Atocha; Mon–Sun 7.30am–1pm, 5.30pm–9pm; free). The Virgin of Atocha is much revered in Madrid.

REAL FÁBRICA DE TAPICES

Opposite at calle Fuenterrabía No. 2, a slim chimney rises from the brick and rubblework building of the **Real Fábrica de Tapices** ❾ (Royal Tapestry Factory; www.realfabricadetapices.com; Mon–Fri 10am–2pm; guided tours only, in English at 1pm). The factory has been on this site since the end of the 19th century but was founded in 1720 by Felipe V.

Turning right then right again from the factory brings you to the Avenida de la Ciudad de Barcelona, where you can take the metro from Menéndez Pelayo station back to Puerta del Sol.

Food and Drink

❶ RODILLA

Calle de Alcalá 67; tel: 91 7555322; www.rodilla.es; Mon–Fri 7am–10pm, Sat–Sun 9am–9pm; €

There are branches all over town of this handy, reasonably priced sandwich shop, which has been going since 1939. There is a wide range available and you can eat in or take away.

❷ FLORIDA RETIRO

Paseo República de Panamá, Parque del Retiro; tel: 91 8275275, www.floridaretiro.com; Mon–Wed and Sun 10am–midnight, Thu–Sun 10am–6am; €€

Sit down for a drink, snack or meal in this attractive conservatory-style gastrobar and restaurant. The mozzarella, mortadella and truffle toasted sandwich is good with a beer. There are evening shows in an adjoining venue.

PLAZA DE SANTA ANA AND THE BARRIO DE LAS LETRAS

The characterful area around Plaza de Santa Ana, known as the Barrio de Las Letras – the Literary Quarter – was where Madrid's first theatres emerged at the end of the 16th century. A vibrant, arty vibe pervades the streets to this day.

TIME: Two hours
DISTANCE: 2km (1.25 miles)
START/END: Plaza de Santa Ana
POINTS TO NOTE: It is fun to do this walk in the early evening, maybe after the Thyssen-Bornemisza or Prado museums, stopping off at tapas bars.

The area is now full of bars and independent boutiques, but for centuries poets, playwrights and novelists lived in this triangle of narrow streets, many of which are named after famous literary figures. Although not much survives from Spain's Golden Age in the 17th century, as you walk around it is easy to imagine the intrigues that took place here.

PLAZA DE SANTA ANA

The focal point of the neighbourhood filled with pavement cafés, the **Plaza de Santa Ana** ❶ was created when a large convent was demolished in the 19th century. Dominating the square at the eastern end is the neoclassical **Teatro Español**, Madrid's most important theatre. It has evolved into this grand building from its origins as the Corral del Príncipe, a simple wooden playhouse in a courtyard, where plays by the luminaries of the Golden Age were staged every afternoon. A statue of the poet and playwright Federico García Lorca (1898–1936) in front of the theatre is a popular meeting point.

At the other end of the square, a large marble statue of the playwright Pedro Calderón (1600–81), one of the most renowned Golden Age dramatists, stands in front of the sparkling white ME Madrid hotel (see page 94). Looking as if it has been transported from a genteel spa resort, with its turret topped with a spherical beacon, it was previously the Hotel Reina Victoria –a favourite of bullfighters, particularly Manolete.

The most famous of the many bars on the square is the **Cervecería Alemana** at No. 6, see ❶, where Ernest Hemingway used to meet up with bullfighting friends in the 1950s.

The Teatro Español dominates the Plaza de Santa Ana

CALLE DEL PRADO

Leave the square at the southeast corner and walk down calle del Prado, where several antique bookshops survive among more modern shops. At No. 21 on the left is the **Ateneo de Madrid** ❷ (www.ateneodemadrid.com), which was founded in 1835 by a group of liberal intellectuals. Although it is a private club, visitors can usually wander in and have a look at the panelled interiors, portrait gallery and library.

Walk back up calle del Prado and turn left into calle León – the name comes from a lion kept in a cage here in the 17th century. On the left, on the corner of calle Cervantes, a plaque marks the site of the house where Miguel de Cervantes, Spain's greatest writer and the author of *Don Quixote*, died in 1616.

Another plaque commemorates the *mentidero de representantes*, the spot where the movers and shakers of the theatrical world – and a large entourage of hangers-on – would meet to see and be seen in the 16th and 17th centuries. At the time, this stretch was a small square with trees, providing just enough space for people to gather and discuss the merits or otherwise of plays, writers, actors and actresses. Members of the theatrical profession came to strike deals and hire people, but of course the main attraction was the opportunity to pick up on the latest scandals.

CASA MUSEO LOPE DE VEGA

Walk down calle Cervantes to No. 11, where the home of the great playwright of the Golden Age, Félix Lope de Vega, is now the **Casa Museo Lope de Vega** ❸ (tel: 91 4299216; http://casamuseolopedevega.org; Tue–Sun 10am–6pm; guided tour, book in advance). Lope de Vega lived here from 1610 until his death in 1635 at the age of 73. He is thought to have written 1,500 plays, as well as novels and poetry, drawing on the many dramas, tragedies and passionate affairs in his life. His works are just as relevant today and are frequently performed throughout Spain.

Although very few of the playwright's belongings have survived, the

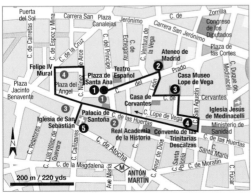

Barlife in calle de las Huertas

museum is a good recreation of a home of the time; it is austerely decorated with furniture of the period and set around a peaceful courtyard garden.

Across the street from the museum, walk up the short calle Quevedo. A plaque on the corner with calle Lope de Vega indicates where the poet and satirist Francisco de Quevedo (1580–1645) once lived, after evicting his arch rival Luis de Góngora.

CONVENTO DE LAS TRINITARIAS DESCALZAS

Opposite, on calle Lope de Vega, is the 17th-century **Convento de las Trinitarias Descalzas** ❹ (Convent of the Barefoot Trinitarians). A few nuns still live in the massive convent, which is not open to the public. In the church, a stone tablet commemorates that Cervantes was buried there, although it is unclear whether the tomb is still there or not. Walking down calle Lope de Vega and turning right into calle de Las Trinitarias, you can see that an entire block is taken up by the austere brick façade of the convent.

CALLE DE LAS HUERTAS

Turn right up calle de las Huertas, a pedestrianised street lined with bars, and on the pavement, quotes by authors including Galdós and Cervantes are set into the paving stones in brass letters.

The neoclassical building on the left on the corner with calle León was designed by Juan de Villanueva in 1788 and houses the **Real Academia de la Historia** (Royal History Academy). It was built for the monks of El Escorial (see page 82), who printed and sold their prayer books here.

On the right, on the corner of calle del Príncipe, the **Palacio de Santoña** is now the Chamber of Commerce and Industry. Built in 1734 by Pedro de Ribera, it features one of his typically elaborate Baroque doorways.

Opposite is the **Casa Alberto** tavern, see ❷, with a red wooden frontage, which is a good spot for a drink. In the early 17th century, Cervantes lived for a while at a house on this site.

IGLESIA DE SAN SEBASTIÁN

At the end of calle de las Huertas, a florist's now stands on the site of the cemetery of the adjacent **Iglesia de San Sebastián** ❺ (Mon–Sat 9.30am–1pm, 6–8.30pm, Sun 9.30am–1.45pm, 6–8.30pm; free). The olive tree remains as a tribute to the literary and theatrical figures who were buried here, including Lope de Vega, whose remains were later moved elsewhere. The church was rebuilt in the mid-20th century after being almost totally destroyed in the Civil War.

Calle de las Huertas opens out into the Plaza del Ángel. On the left is the **Café Central**, see ❸, which is a leading venue for live jazz and other music at night and a good place for a drink or a meal at any time.

The Iglesia de San Sebastián

Take the first right from the square, where the Corral de la Cruz, one of Madrid's first theatres, was set up in a courtyard surrounded by galleried tenements in the late-16th century. A large mural portrays a confused Philip IV, searching in vain for the theatre that was a focus of social life during his reign – and where he had a notorious affair with one of the leading actresses of the day, La Calderona.

The callejón de Álvarez Gato on the right is named after a 15th-century poet. The mirrors along this alley commemorate the spot where two charac-ters in Ramón del Valle-Inclán's play *Luces de Bohemia* (Bohemian Lights, 1924) stand in front of the concave, convex and normal mirrors of an iron-monger's that used to be situated here and comment on the similarity between their distorted reflections and the way writers and artists portray society.

Las Bravas, see ❹, on the left claims to be the place where *patatas bravas* were invented. At the end of the alley, look at the colourful tiled wall of Villa Rosa (www.tablaoflamencovillarosa.com), a famous flamenco club. From the corner, turn right to arrive back in the Plaza de Santa Ana.

Food and Drink

❶ CERVECERÍA ALEMANA

Plaza de Santa Ana 6; www.cerveceriaale mana.com; tel: 91 4297033; Mon, Wed–Sun 11am–12.30am, Fri–Sat until 2am; €

With marble tables and waiters in white jackets, this bar has changed little since it was founded in 1904. It is a popular spot for breakfast, a coffee or a beer with some tapas. The fried fish dishes are excellent.

❷ CASA ALBERTO

Calle Huertas 18; www.casaalberto.es; tel: 91 4299356; Tue–Sat noon–1.30am, Sun noon–4pm; €€

This characterful tapas bar and restaurant has been going for nearly two centuries. Order a draught vermouth and try the lamb sweetbreads and the braised oxtail.

❸ CAFÉ CENTRAL

Plaza del Ángel 10; www.cafecentralmadrid. com; tel: 91 3694143; Mon–Fri 12.30pm–2.30am, Sat–Sun 11.30am–2.30am; €

There is live music most nights at this charac-terful café. They serve drinks and food all day, as well as a good-value set lunch. In the afternoon, come here to read with a coffee.

❹ LAS BRAVAS

Callejón Álvarez Gato 3 (also calle Espoz y Mina 13); tel: 91 5228581; https://lasbravas.com; Mon–Sun 12.30–4.30pm, 7–11.30pm; €

You may have tried a lot of *patatas bravas*, but the original recipe was invented in the 1930s in this no-nonsense bar with orange décor in tribute to the famous fiery sauce. Share a portion with a cold beer or two and try the fried pig's ear too if you are feeling adventurous.

Stall at the El Rastro street market

THE RASTRO MARKET AND LAVAPIÉS

This walk, which explores the characterful streets sloping down from the Plaza Mayor, is more about traditions than sights. On Sunday mornings, crowds flock to the Rastro flea market, which is a real institution in the city.

DISTANCE: 3km (2 miles)
TIME: Half a day
START: Plaza de Cascorro
END: La Casa Encendida
POINTS TO NOTE: Although the market only takes place on Sundays (until 3pm), this is an interesting area to explore at any time. Beware, theft is rife.

Lavapiés was the Jewish quarter until the end of the 15th century. The area is now the most multicultural in Madrid, with new inhabitants from North Africa, Asia and the Far East and a proliferation of ethnic restaurants.

THE RASTRO

Dive into the throng at the **Plaza de Cascorro ❶** at the top of calle Ribera de Curtidores. On Sunday mornings, the area buzzes with stalls selling bags, books and much more. Just as interesting, however, are the vintage shops open all week..

Bear right along calle Amazonas to Plaza General Vara de Rey, filled on market day with antiques and second-hand clothes. Turn left down calle Carlos Arniches. On the left at No. 3 is the **Centro Cultural La Corrala** (Mon–Fri 10am–8pm, Sat 10am–2pm; free), one of Madrid's oldest surviving examples of balconied dwellings set around a courtyard.

At the bottom of the hill is **El Capricho Extremeño**, see ❶, if you want a snack. Head to Plaza Campillo Mundo Nuevo, then turn left back up Ribera de Curtidores.

IGLESIA DE SAN CAYETANO

Turn right along calle San Cayetano to calle Embajadores and the **Iglesia de**

Food and Drink

❶ EL CAPRICHO EXTREMEÑO
Calle Carlos Arniches 30; tel: 91 3655841; Sat–Sun 8.30am–4.30pm; €
This place only opens at weekends to serve slabs of toast with tasty toppings including prawns, octopus, ham and cheese. Another branch at calle Toledo 21 is open all week.

La Corrala is an example of galleried buildings typical of the Lavapiés district

San Cayetano ➋ (Mon–Sat 9am–noon, 6–8pm, Sun 9am–2pm, 6–8pm; free). The pink brick façade dates to the late-17th century but was rebuilt in the 1960s.

Further down on the left is **Plaza Arturo Barea ➌**, renamed in 2017 in homage to the author of *The Forging of a Rebel*. On the right is the **Mercado de San Fernando** (Mon–Fri 9am–2.15pm, 5–8pm, Sat 9am–2.30pm) food market. The large brick structure next door is the 18th-century **Escuelas Pías de San Fernando**, home to the city's Open University.

LA CORRALA

The pink building at the end of the square, known simply as **La Corrala**, is a National Monument. It is the most famous example of the galleried buildings typical of this district.

PLAZA DE LAVAPIÉS

At the end of calle Sombrerete is **Plaza de Lavapiés ➍**, once the centre of the medieval Jewish quarter, and still a hub today with its **Teatro Valle-Inclán** (http://cdn.mcu.es/el-cdn/valle-inclan).

From here, head down calle Valencia to ronda de Valencia, where on the right at No. 2 is **La Casa Encendida ➎** (www.lacasaencendida.es; Tue–Sun 10am–10pm; free), a dynamic cultural centre in a neo-Mudéjar building that stages exhibitions, performances and concerts.

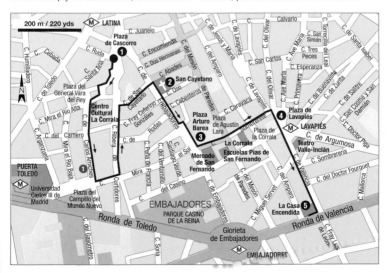

The Mercado de San Antón

CHUECA, MALASAÑA AND CONDE DUQUE

On this route through the lively barrios north of the Gran Vía, full of bars, boutiques and pretty buildings with flower-filled balconies, you see how modern trends have given traditional Madrid a new lease of life.

DISTANCE: 2.5km (1.5 miles)
TIME: Three hours
START: Plaza del Rey
END: Centro Cultural Conde Duque
POINTS TO NOTE: Do this walk in the early evening for the best atmosphere. It links well with routes 1 and 10 or with shopping on calle Fuencarral.

The three neighbourhoods explored on this route have distinct characters: fashionable Chueca is Madrid's main gay area; bohemian Malasaña has smartened up and is now as popular in the day as it is at night, while elegant Conde Duque has a less frantic, more cultural vibe. Along the way, there are some interesting museums, galleries and churches, as well as lots of cafés and shops.

PLAZA DEL REY

Our walk starts near Plaza de Cibeles on **Plaza del Rey ❶**. The square is dominated by the Ministerio de Cultura (Ministry of Culture), which has annexed the

restored **Casa de la Siete Chimeneas**, named after its seven chimneys. One of the oldest buildings in the city, it dates back to 1577 and is rumoured to be haunted. The steel abstract sculpture is by Eduardo Chillida and the statue is of Lieutenant Jacinto Ruiz, one of the heroes of the 1808 battle against the French.

Walk up calle Barquillo, looking up at the glassed-in balconies, and turn left into calle Augusto Figueroa, lined with outlet shoe shops. Have a look in the **Mercado de San Antón**, see ❶, a gastromarket on several floors. Or if you just fancy an ice cream, pop up the street to **Mistura**, see ❷.

Opposite the market, cut through to the **Plaza de Chueca ❷**, the heart of the neighbourhood with its many café terraces. At the end of the square is one of Madrid's most traditional taverns, the **Taberna de Ángel Sierra**, see ❸.

SOCIEDAD GENERAL DE AUTORES

Walk up calle Gravina and turn right into calle Pelayo. At the end, on the corner of calle Fernando VI, is the extraordi-

Sociedad General de Autores

Inside the charming Museo del Romanticismo

nary sight of the **Sociedad General de Autores ❸** (Performing Rights Society), where strange forms of plant life seem to be oozing out of the walls. The building, designed in 1902 by Catalan architect José Grases Riera, is the best example of Art Nouveau architecture in Madrid.

Continue along calle Fernando VI, which becomes calle Mejía Lequerica. Crossing over, there is a great olive oil shop on the corner, Patrimonio Comunal Olivarero, then on the first block on the left is the **Casa de los Lagartos** (House of the Lizards). Look up to see the stone lizards 'holding up' the cornice.

MUSEO DEL ROMANTICISMO

Take the first left along calle San Mateo, where on the right at No. 13 is the **Museo del Romanticismo ❹** (Museum of Romanticism; www.mecd.gob.es/mro-manticismo; Tue–Sat 9.30am–6.30pm, May–Oct until 8.30pm, Sun 10am–3pm; free Sat after 2pm). This charming museum gives a fascinating insight into the Romantic Movement, when artists and writers began to explore free expression, which emerged in Spain in the 1820s. This was the house of the Marquis of Vega-Inclán (1845–1942), who was a leading exponent of the movement. Highlights include paintings by Goya and 19th-century artists including Leonardo Alenza. One room is devoted to the satirist Mariano Jose de Larra, who shot himself at the age of 28 following a doomed love affair.

MUSEO DE LA HISTORIA DE MADRID

Continue along calle San Mateo and turn right onto calle Fuencarral, which is lined with boutiques. On your right is the **Museo de la Historia de Madrid ❺** (Museum of the History of Madrid; www.madrid.es/museodehistoria; Tue–Sun 10am–7pm, mid-Sept–June until 8pm; free). Originally an orphanage, the building was designed by Pedro de Ribera in the 18th century. The displays chart Madrid's development from medieval time to the 20th century (earlier history is dealt with at the Museo de San Isidro, see page 35). It is worth going in just to see the extraordinary wooden scale model of Madrid made in 1830 by León Gil de Palacio.

MALASAÑA

Opposite the museum, walk down calle San Vicente Ferrer. You are now in Malasaña, a neighbourhood of red-brick apartment blocks built at the turn of the 20th century with an abundance of bars and independent shops. The area gets its name from Manuela Malasaña, a teenage seamstress who was a heroine of the uprising against Napoleon's troops, which took place nearby on 2 May 1808.

Turn right down calle San Andrés. On the left, look at the tiled walls from a former pharmacy, which were made in 1920 and show miracle cures for whooping cough and tuberculosis.

Plaza del Dos de Mayo, with the two marble statues of Velarde and Daoíz

PLAZA DEL DOS DE MAYO

At the bottom of the hill is the **Plaza del Dos de Mayo ⑥**. Desperate Madrilenians tried to arm themselves with weapons stored in an artillery barracks that stood here. The monument in the square commemorates Captains Pedro Velarde and Luís Daoíz, who led the defence and died in the fighting. The atmosphere is much more peaceful now, with plenty of places to stop for a drink or a bite to eat, including **Cabreira**, see ④, which has outdoor tables.

From the square, walk down Calle Daoíz, which leads to calle San Bernardo. On the right is the **Convento de las Salesas de Nuestra Señora de la Visitación** (9.30am–1.30pm, 4–8pm; free) where you can buy biscuits made by the nuns at the entrance.

On the opposite side of calle San Bernardo is the **Iglesia de Santa María la Real de Montserrat** (Mon–Sun 7.30am–10.30am, 7pm–9pm; free). Its Baroque tower was designed by Pedro de Ribera in the 18th century.

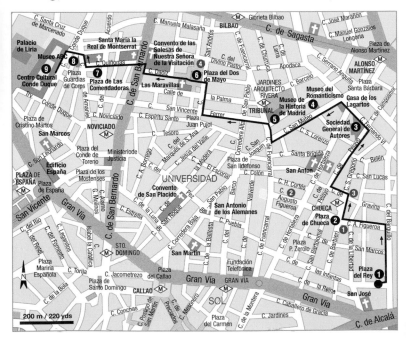

Exhibition at Centro Cultural Conde Duque

PLAZA DE LAS COMENDADORAS

Walk along calle Quiñones, by the side of the church, to the tranquil **Plaza de las Comendadoras ❼** in the pleasant Conde Duque neighbourhood. Taking up the entire right side of the square is the **Convento de las Comendadoras de Santiago** (tel: 91 5481842; guided tours 1st and 3rd Mon of each month, 3.30pm–6.30pm). Built in the 17th and 18th centuries for the nuns protected by the knights of the Order of Santiago (St James), the convent was designed by Sabatini and the church by Manuel and José del Olmo.

Turn right out of the square up calle Amaniel to reach the **Museo ABC ❽** (http://museo.abc.es; Tue–Sat 11am–8pm, Sun 10am–2pm; free), a museum devoted to drawing, illustration and graphic design. The museum is housed in an old brewery redesigned by Spanish architects, Aranguren and Gallegos.

CENTRO CULTURAL CONDE DUQUE

Just above the museum, turn left into calle Montserrat, which leads to the **Centro Cultural Conde Duque ❾** (http://conde duquemadrid.es; Tue–Sat 10am–2pm, 5.30–9pm, Sun 10.30am–2pm; exhibitions usually free), set in the former barracks of the Royal Guard. Designed by Pedro de Ribera in 1717, with one of his trademark Baroque entrances, it is now used for exhibitions as well as film, theatre and dance.

Food and Drink

❶ MERCADO DE SAN ANTÓN

Calle Augusto Figueroa 24; tel: 91 3300730; Mon–Sun 10am–midnight; €
Chueca's neighbourhood food market has been rebuilt to suit modern tastes with gourmet stalls, tapas places and a bar and restaurant up on the roof terrace.

❷ MISTURA

Calle Augusto Figueroa 5; tel: 91 7556391; http://misturaicecream.com; Mon–Sun 8am–11am, Fri–Sat until midnight; €
The founders of this artisan shop and café use methods learned in India to create delicious ice creams with no artificial ingredients. Good juices and coffee too.

❸ TABERNA DE ÁNGEL SIERRA

Calle Gravina 11; tel: 91 5310126; Mon–Sun 11am–2.30am; €
Founded in 1917, the tavern has a tiled interior and a zinc bar. The beer and draught vermouth are excellent, accompanied by simple tapas.

❹ CABREIRA

Calle Ruíz 2, Plaza Dos de Mayo; tel: 91 593 0200; www.cabreira.es; Tue–Sat 10am–1am, Sun 11am–8pm; €
You can have a beer at the bar, tapas or a full meal. Try the *patatas a la churri* – fried potatoes with scrambled egg, onion and garlic. There is another branch nearby at calle Velarde 13, which is open Mondays.

Homage to Cervantes in Plaza de España

FROM PLAZA DE ESPAÑA TO THE CASA DE CAMPO

Exploring the west of Madrid takes you to a quirky museum, an Egyptian temple and a church with Goya frescoes, before walking along the newly-developed banks of the Manzanares river to the city's biggest park.

DISTANCE: 4km (2.5 miles)
TIME: Half a day
START: Plaza de España
END: Casa de Campo
POINTS TO NOTE: You could vary this route, taking the cable car and going to the zoo and funfair, to make it more child-friendly. It combines well with the latter parts of routes 9 and 11.

This route is less urban than most of the others, going mostly through parkland. In the Casa de Campo, you almost feel like you are in the countryside, so this is a good walk to do to clear your head after a few days in the busy city centre.

PLAZA DE ESPAÑA

The large, landscaped **Plaza de España** ❶ at the end of the Gran Vía is undergoing a long redevelopment process to make it a more attractive leisure area. In the centre is a monument to Cervantes, preceded by statues of Don Quixote and Sancho Panza, sculpted by Coullaut Valera in 1915.

Taking up the top of the square is the colossal **Edificio España**, a typical example of the grand-scale architecture of Franco's dictatorship. Completed in 1953, it was the tallest building in Spain at the time. Designed by Joaquín and Julián Otamendi, the 26-storey building is undergoing extensive rebuilding to house a hotel, but over the decades has been occupied by offices, flats, shops and restaurants and has almost functioned as a mini-town in its own right.

The Otamendi brothers were also responsible for the 32-storey **Torre de Madrid** on the north side of the square, built four years later. The Barceló Torre de Madrid hotel (see page 96) now occupies the first nine floors, with flats and offices above.

Just off the square to the northwest is the **Palacio de Liria** (Calle Princesa 20; www.fundacioncasadealba.com; visits Fri 10am, 11am and noon with prior online reservation). The 18th-century palace belongs to the House of Alba and contains an astounding art collection, with works by Goya and Titian, but public

Museo Cerralbo interior

The iconic Edificio España

access is strictly limited and you have to book a place months in advance.

MUSEO CERRALBO

Walk down to the bottom of Plaza de España and turn right up calle Ferraz. On the first corner on the right is the **Museo Cerralbo ②** (calle Ventura Rodriguez 17; tel: 91 547 3646; (www.mecd.gob.es/mcerralbo; Tue–Sat 9.30am–3pm, Thu also 5pm–8pm, Sun 10am–3pm; free Sat after 2pm, Thu after 5pm, Sun). Housed in the grand residence of its founder, Enrique de Aguilera y Gamboa, the Marquis of Cerralbo, this fascinating museum gives an insight into aristocratic life in Madrid in the late 19th and early 20th centuries. The

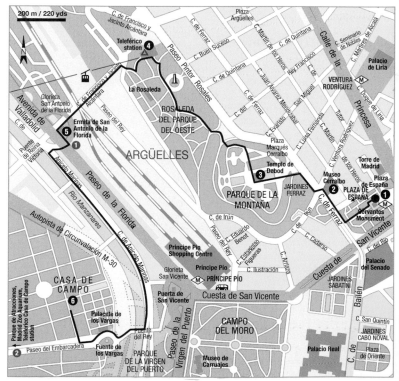

The Templo de Debod looks its best lit up at night

Marquis was an eccentric character who travelled widely, bringing all sorts of objects back from his trips. He was also a keen archaeologist and was active in the political life of the time. Exhibits include paintings by Titian, Zurbarán and El Greco, as well as ceramics, swords and tapestries. Several rooms are decorated pretty much how they must have been when the family lived there, including the music room, library and opulent ballroom.

TEMPLO DE DEBOD

Return to calle Ferraz and cross the road to reach the **Parque del Oeste** (West Park) on the hill opposite. On the right is the somewhat surprising sight of the **Templo de Debod ❸** (Debod Temple; www.esmadrid.com/en/tourist-information/templo-de-debod; Tue–Fri Apr–Sept 10am–2pm, 6pm–8pm, Oct–Mar 9.45am–1.45pm, 4.15pm–6.15pm, Sat–Sun (all year) 10am–2pm; free). The temple was given to Spain in 1968 in thanks for the work of Spanish archaeologists who had helped salvage the temples of Abu Simbel, which would otherwise have been flooded as a result of the construction of the Aswan Dam on the Nile. More than 2,000 years old, it was rebuilt stone by stone, and still faces east-west, as it did originally.

Walking north through the park, on the left is the **Rosaleda** garden, where around 600 varieties of rose are grown. Just beyond it is the **Teleférico** station **❹** (www.teleferico.com), where you can take a cable car ride over to the Casa de Campo park, which is worth doing for the views alone.

Walk down the steps by the station and continue down the path through the park, passing a small cemetery containing the common grave of the victims shot near here by the French on 3 May 1808. Goya's painting of this tragic event is in the Prado Museum (see page 48).

ERMITA DE SAN ANTONIO DE LA FLORIDA

Cross the bridge over the railway tracks to reach the **Ermita de San Antonio de la Florida ❺** (Glorieta de San Antonio de la Florida 5; Tue–Sun 9.30am–8pm, guided tours Mon–Fri 9.30am–1pm; free).

Saint Anthony's day

On 13 June, the feast day of St Anthony, hundreds of women of all ages take part in one of Madrid´s more curious customs, thought to have been started by seamstresses. The saint is apparently able to rustle up lovers for anyone who might require one – or more. The hopeful participants have to drop 13 pins into the church font, which is taken outside into the garden to accommodate the crowds, then put the palm of their hand on top to see how many stick to it. The number of pins that stick indicates the number of boyfriends they can expect to come along in the year to come.

Cable car over Casa de Campo, one of the biggest parks in Europe

The dome of this neoclassical church is decorated with frescoes that were painted by Goya in 1798. He completed the work in only four months, which impressed Carlos IV so much that Goya was appointed court painter. The frescoes depict Saint Anthony, who brings a murdered man back to life to declare the innocence of the saint's father, who had been accused of the crime. A crowd of people with expressive faces are observing the scene, leaning on a rail around the cupola,

Underneath the dome is Goya's tomb, erected in 1919 when his remains were brought from Bordeaux, where he died in 1828. A replica chapel was built alongside in the 1920s for parish services to aid the preservation of the frescoes.

Next to the chapel is **Casa Mingo**, see ❶, an Asturian tavern and a Madrid institution. Walk south along the bank of the Manzanares river, where a redevelopment scheme begun at the beginning of the 21st century, known as **Madrid Río**, has resulted in this part of the city becoming a popular leisure area.

On the left, part of the Príncipe Pio train station, originally called the Estación del Norte, is now a large shopping centre. The arch up ahead is the **Puerta de San Vicente**, a replica of the original designed in the 18th century by Sabatini.

CASA DE CAMPO

Cross the road over to the **Casa de Campo** ❻. Now one of the biggest parks in Europe, it was created by Felipe II in the mid-16th century as a hunting ground near the Alcázar palace. The path ahead leads to the boating lake, bordered by restaurants with terrace tables. One of the best spots overlooking the water is **La Parrilla del Embarcadero**, see ❷.

Facilities in the park include an outdoor swimming pool and a pleasant modern **zoo** (www.zoomadrid.com; hours vary, usually 10.30am until dusk) and the **Parque de Atracciones** funfair (www.parquedeatracciones.es; hours vary, usually noon until late evening).

You can take the metro back to the city centre from Lago station, near the lake, or get the Teleférico cable car.

Food and Drink

❶ CASA MINGO

Paseo de la Florida 2; tel: 91 5477918; www.casamingo.es; Mon–Sun 11am–midnight; €
Open since 1888, this very popular restaurant with outdoor tables specialises in Asturian cooking with spit-roast chicken, Cabrales blue cheese and cider brewed on the premises. Takeaway available.

❷ LA PARRILLA DEL EMBARCADERO

Paseo del Embarcadero; tel: 91 463 1024; http://laparrilladelembarcadero.es; Mon–Sun 10am–10.30pm; €€
There are lovely views of the lake at this friendly restaurant, which specialises in grilled meats.

Cuartel General del Aire, the headquarters of the Spanish air force

AROUND MONCLOA

It is worth going to the area around Madrid's main university to get off the tourist beat and visit the important Museo de América before relaxing in the delightful Parque del Oeste.

> **DISTANCE:** 5km (3 miles)
> **TIME:** Half a day
> **START:** Cuartel General del Aire
> **END:** Plaza de España
> **POINTS TO NOTE:** You can link this with route 10 when you get to the park, although this will involve a lot of walking if you visit all the sights along the way.

The Moncloa area spreads out around the top of calle Princesa, the shopping street that leads up from the Plaza de España. A key location in the Civil War, it has several examples of the mock-Habsburg architecture and triumphal monuments that were built after the conflict. Nowadays, the thousands of students who attend the sprawling university mean there is always a lively, laidback atmosphere.

MONCLOA

Take the metro to Moncloa station, a hub for buses around the Madrid region and to Segovia. You emerge on calle Princesa by the immense **Cuartel General del Aire** ❶, the headquarters of the Spanish air force. Built in the 1940s by Luis Gutiérrez Soto, the Habsburg-style building has slate roofs and slender spires.

This area is the access point to the **Universidad Complutense** campus to the northwest. The university was founded in Alcalá de Henares by Cardinal Cisneros in 1499 and transferred to Madrid in 1936, originally on calle San Bernardo before the sprawling complex was built in the second half of the 20th century.

Up ahead is the **Arco de la Victoria** ❷, a triumphal arch that commemorates General Franco's military victory on taking control of Madrid in the Civil War in 1939.

FARO DE MONCLOA

Cross Calle Princesa, passing a circular temple built as a monument to Franco's soldiers who died in the conflict, but is now used by the City Council. Follow the stream of students heading up the path on the left to reach the **Faro de Moncloa** ❸ (Moncloa Lighthouse; www.esmadrid.com/faro-de-moncloa; Tue–Sun

View of Madrid from the Faro del Moncloa

9.30am–8pm). This telecommunications' tower, which is 92 metres (300 ft) high, has a circular observation deck with panoramic views across Madrid to the Sierra de Guadarrama. Next to the university campus, look for the Palacio de la Moncloa, the official residence of the Spanish prime minister.

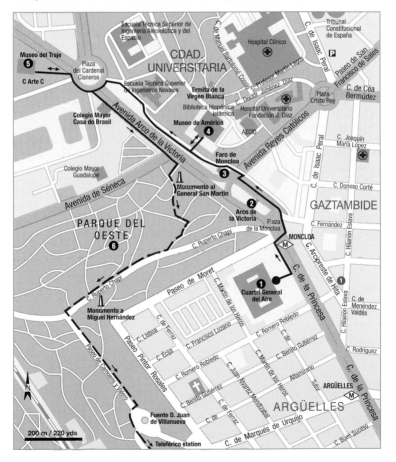

Los Mulatos de Esmeraldas can be seen at the Museo de América

MUSEO DE ÁMERICA

Immediately adjacent is the **Museo de América ➍** (Museum of America; www.mecd.gob.es/museodeamerica; Tue–Sat 9.30am–3pm, Thu until 7pm, Sun 9.30am–3pm; free Thu after 2pm, Sun). The large museum deals with the ancient civilisations and cultures of Spain's former colonies in Latin America, with superlative collections of art, ceramics, maps, jewellery and sacred objects. Highlights include the Quimbayas Treasure from Colombia, dating from AD 500–1,000, and the Tro-Cortesian Codex, which is one of only four Mayan manuscripts in the world.

MUSEO DEL TRAJE

It is a 10-minute walk up the Avenida de la Memoria (or take bus Nos. 46 or 160) to the **Museo del Traje CIPE ➎** (Clothing Museum and Ethnological Heritage Research Centre; Avenida Juan de Herrera 2; www.mecd.gob.es/mtraje; Tue–Sat 9.30am–7pm, Sun 10am–3pm; free Sat after 2.30pm and Sun). The museum charts the development of what people have been wearing from the late 16th century to current times. Exhibits include Spanish regional costumes and clothes by leading 20th and 21st century Spanish designers, including Balenciaga and Paco Rabanne. There is a good café as well as a book and gift shop.

Return to Moncloa. If you feel like an ice cream, head to **Los Alpes**, see ➊, before going into the **Parque del Oeste ➏** on the right – unless you are in the mood for shopping, in which case just walk down Calle Princesa with its boutiques and El Corte Inglés department store.

PARQUE DEL OESTE

The lovely L-shaped park slopes from Moncloa down towards Plaza de España and the Manzanares river. It was designed at the beginning of the 20th-century by the landscape gardener Cecilio Rodríguez but had to be replanted after suffering severe damage during the Civil War. It was also the scene of fighting in the 1808 uprising against the French. If you follow the calle Ruperto Chapí down to the Glorieta del Maestro, then turn left along the Paseo de Camoens, you emerge on the Paseo del Pintor Rosales, where you can sit at one of the pavement cafés before continuing towards Plaza de España. This final part of the park is covered in route 10.

Food and Drink

➊ LOS ALPES

Calle Arcipreste de Hita 6; tel: 91 5439446; www.heladeriaslosalpes.es; Mon–Sun 10am–10pm
This family-run place opened in 1950 and serves around 50 varieties of homemade ice cream. The most popular is *mantecado*, made with egg yolk.

Puerta de Europa, rising up above busy Plaza de Castilla

THE PASEO DE LA CASTELLANA

A showcase of 20th and 21st century architecture, the Paseo de la Castellana is the city's main north–south axis, stretching for 5km (3 miles) from the Plaza de Colón with a string of superb museums along the way.

DISTANCE: 5km (3 miles)
TIME: Half a day
START: Plaza de Colón
END: Plaza de Castilla
POINTS TO NOTE: It is a good idea to use the No. 27 bus up the Paseo de la Castellana, for at least part of the route. If you visit all the museums, you will need a full day.

The Plaza de Colón marks the start of the Paseo de la Castellana. The busy boulevard was begun in the reign of Fernando VII but was not really established until the second half of the 19th century when it was extended as far as the Plaza San Juan de la Cruz. By the early 20th century, the new avenue was lined with palaces, most of which have been supplanted by sleek office buildings.

PLAZA DE COLÓN

The **Plaza de Colón** ❶ honours Christopher Columbus and the discovery of America. In the centre is the neo-Gothic Columbus monument, while the three abstract blocks in the pedestrianised square – the **Jardines del Descubrimiento** (Discovery Gardens) – represent Columbus's ships. Behind the cascade of water on the west side is the **Teatro Fernán Gómez – Centro Cultural de la Villa** (www.teatrofernangomez.es), a municipal theatre and cultural centre.

East of the square is the elegant Salamanca district, devised by the flamboyant Marquis of Salamanca and built between 1860 and 1920. Now Goya, Serrano and adjoining streets are Madrid's smartest shopping area (see 21).

The south side of the square is taken up by the **Biblioteca Nacional de España** (National Library of Spain; www.bne.es; Tue–Sat 10am–8pm, Sun 10am–2pm; free). Designed by Francisco Jareño in the second half of the 19th century, it has a museum and holds temporary exhibitions.

MUSEO ARQUEOLÓGICO NACIONAL

The rear of the library building (entrance on calle Serrano) is occupied by the

The Lady of Elche, Museo Arqueológico Nacional

Museo Arqueológico Nacional (National Archaeological Museum; http://www. man.es; Tue–Sat 9.30am–8pm, Sun 9.30am–3pm; free Sat after 2pm and Sun), one of the most important museums in Spain. Allow at least two hours as there is a lot to see, including the Lady of Elche, a masterpiece of Iberian sculpture from the late 5th or early 6th century BC. The extraordinary Visigothic Guarrazar Treasure includes Recceswinth's bejewelled votive crown. There are also Roman mosaics, Muslim decorative arts and finds from ancient Egypt and Greece. Outside, you'll find a replica of the Altamira caves in Cantabria.

Opposite the Biblioteca Nacional, at Paseo de Recoletos No. 41, is the **Museo de Cera** (Wax Museum; http://museoceramadrid.com; Mon–Fri 10am–2.30pm, 4.30–8.30pm, Sat–Sun 10am–8.30pm), with waxworks of Picasso, Tom Cruise and Rafael Nadal. The twin towers on the northwest corner of Plaza de Colón, linked at the top by what looks like a green hat, are the **Torres Heron**, designed by Antonio Lamela in the 1970s.

Before heading up the Paseo de la Castellana, you might want to stop at **Platea Madrid**, see ❶, on the northeast side of the square, for some refreshment.

PASEO DE LA CASTELLANA

Walking north up the central boulevard of the Paseo de la Castellana, on the right at No. 34 is the **ABC building** with its Andalusian-tiled façade. Now

Museo Lázaro Galdiano   *Painting at the Museo Sorolla*

a shopping centre, it was originally the headquarters of the *ABC* newspaper.

Under the flyover nearby are some sculptures – rather grandly called the **Museo de Esculturas al Aire Libre** ❷ (Museum of Open-air Sculpture) – where the stand-out work is the cement *Stranded Mermaid* by Eduardo Chillida.

MUSEO SOROLLA

Two blocks further up, at the Glorieta de Emilio Castelar junction, turn left up Paseo General Martinez Campos, where at No. 37 on the right is the charming **Museo Sorolla** ❸ (www.mecd.gob.es/msorolla; Tue–Sat 9.30am–8pm, Sun 10am–3pm; free Sat after 2pm and Sun).

Joaquín Sorolla was born in Valencia in 1863 and lived in this house from 1911 until his death in 1923. Even if you don't recognise his name, you may well be familiar with some of his languid beach scenes. Sorolla's studio is still pretty much how it was when he lived here and contains some of his best-known paintings. Also on display are some of the works he painted for the Hispanic Society of America in New York, which depict people from all over Spain in traditional dress. Sorolla was also responsible for the lovely garden, inspired by the Alhambra in Granada and the Reales Alcazares in Seville.

Returning to the Paseo de la Castellana, cross over to the corner of calle General Oraá. If it is time for lunch, the **BiBo** brasserie, see ❷, on the left is a good option.

MUSEO LÁZARO GALDIANO

Walk up calle General Oraá and turn left onto calle Serrano. On your right is the **Museo Lázaro Galdiano** ❹ (www.flg.es; Tue–Sat 10am–4.30pm, Sun 10am–3pm; free last hour), which holds one of Madrid's most interesting private art collections but is never crowded. The museum is housed in the Italianate palatial residence of publisher and businessman José Lázaro Galdiano (1862–1947), who was an enthusiastic patron of the arts. The extensive displays range from paintings to jewellery and antiques, with works by Bosch, Gainsborough, Rembrandt, Velázquez, Zurbarán, El Greco and Goya.

Turn right out of the museum and left along calle María de Molina to get back to the Paseo de la Castellana.

MUSEO NACIONAL DE CIENCIAS NATURALES

Next up on the right is the **Museo Nacional de Ciencias Naturales** ❺ (National Museum of Natural Sciences; www.mncn.csic.es; Tue–Fri 10am–5pm, Sat–Sun 10am–8pm). Housed in a striking late-19th-century building, the museum brings science to life with lots of interactive exhibits to help visitors of all ages learn about evolution and the natural world.

NUEVOS MINISTERIOS

The next stage of the Castellana's development began in the 1930s at the next

The Bernabéu, Real Madrid's home stadium

junction, **Plaza de San Juan de la Cruz**. The entire block on the left it taken up by the **Nuevos Ministerios** ❻ (New Ministries), a complex of government buildings inspired by the austere style of El Escorial .

At the top end the underground Nuevos Ministerios transport hub is where you can get the metro or train to the airport.

Rising up on the left is the high-rise complex **AZCA**, with a huge El Corte Inglés department store. The tallest building is the striking white **Torre Picasso** at 157 metres (515 ft), designed by Minoru Yamasaki.

Further up, the frieze fronting the **Palacio de Congresos** conference centre is the unmistakable work of Joan Miró.

ESTADIO SANTIAGO BERNABÉU

Cross the Castellana to get to the **Estadio Santiago Bernabéu** ❼ (www.realmadrid.com/en/tickets/bernabeu-tour; Mon–Sat 10am–7.30pm, Sun 10.30am–6.30pm except match days, when tours run until five hours before kick-off). The Real Madrid football club was founded in 1902 and this stadium was built in the 1940s, but has since been remodelled. The self-guided tour includes the impressive trophy room, the dressing rooms and press area. You can also walk down the players' tunnel out onto the pitch.

PLAZA DE CASTILLA

From the stadium, jump on a No. 27 or No. 147 bus up the Castellana to the **Plaza de Castilla** ❽, another key trans-

port hub. The white concrete sculpture is a monument to Calvo Sotelo, the Nationalist leader whose assassination in 1936 sparked the Civil War. The obelisk in the centre is by Santiago Calatrava. Dominating the junction are two towers that lean inwards to create the **Puerta de Europa** (Gateway to Europe), marking the start of Madrid's new business area, as evidenced by the skyscrapers rising up behind them, known as the **Cuatro Torres** (Four Towers). The tallest is Norman Foster's 2009 Torre Caja Madrid at 250 metres (820 ft).

To get back downtown, you could either take the bus or Lines 1 or 10 of the metro.

Food and Drink

❶ PLATEA MADRID

Goya 5–7 (Plaza de Colón); tel: 91 577 0025; www.plateamadrid.com; Mon–Sun noon–12.30am, Thu–Sat until 2.30am; €
This gastronomic hub has a wide range of Spanish and international cuisines, from coffee and cake at the Mama Framboise café to fruit to take away at Gold Gourmet.

❷ BIBO

Paseo de la Castellana 52; tel: 91 805 2556; www.grupodanigarcia.com/en/booking/bibo-madrid; Mon–Sun 1pm–midnight; €€
Zingy design and superb food at this bar and brasserie by Dani García, who has two Michelin stars at his restaurant in Marbella. The cherry gazpacho, oxtail brioche and fried fish are particularly tasty.

View across the medieval city of Toledo and the Tagus river

TOLEDO

Approached from Madrid, the medieval city of Toledo is a spectacular sight. High on a granite hill and almost surrounded by the Tagus river, it is packed with monuments, museums and churches. To experience Toledo as its most atmospheric, try to spend an evening there.

DISTANCE: 72km (45 miles)
TIME: A full day
START: Puerta de Bisagra
END: Mercado de San Agustín
POINTS TO NOTE: The train from Puerta de Atocha station takes 30 minutes and the bus takes 90 minutes from Plaza Elíptica station.

A microcosm of Spanish history, over the centuries Toledo has been a Roman fortress, a Visigothic capital and a centre of Muslim culture and learning. In the 11th century, it was reconquered by Alfonso VI and became capital of Castile, with Muslims, Jews and Christians living side by side. The court's transfer to Madrid in 1561 sparked the decline which also conserved its astonishing architectural and artistic heritage.

This route traces an anticlockwise loop from the **Puerta de Bisagra ❶**. Facing the Renaissance gate, you can either walk right along the Paseo de Recaredo to enter through the 11th-century **Puerta de Cambrón ❷**, or take the escalators up the hill and turn right at the top.

Follow the signs to the **Monasterio de San Juan de Los Reyes ❸** (www.sanjuandelosreyes.org; Mon–Sun Oct–May 10am–5.30pm, June–Sept 10am–6.30pm). Founded by the Catholic Monarchs, the late-Gothic structure has a cloister with filigree carvings.

JEWISH QUARTER

Turning right out of the monastery, following calle Reyes Católicos, you enter the *Judería*, the old Jewish district. On the left is the **Sinagoga Santa María la Blanca ❹** (Mon–Sun 10am–2pm and 3.30pm–6pm; summer until 7pm). This singular structure with horseshoe arches was built in the 12th century by Moors for Jews under Christian rule.

At the end of the street is the **Sinagoga del Tránsito ❺**, which houses the **Museo Sefardí** (http://museosefardi.mcu.es; Tue–Sat 9.30am–6pm, Mar–Oct until 7.30pm, Sun 10am–3pm), charting the history of Sephardic Jews. Founded in 1366, it is an excellent example of Mudéjar decoration.

Toledo-steel scissors for sale

EL GRECO

Adjacent is the **Casa Museo del Greco ⑥** (http://museodelgreco.mcu.es; Tue–Sat 9.30am–6pm, Mar–Oct until 7.30pm, Sun 10am–3pm). Despite the name, this house was never home to El Greco, who lived in Toledo from 1577 until his death in 1614, but there is evidence to suggest

he lived nearby. Paintings in the museum include his View of Toledo.

El Greco's masterpiece the *Burial of the Count of Orgáz* is on display in the **Iglesia de Santo Tomé ⑦** (Mon–Sun 10am–5.45pm; Mar–mid-Oct until 6.45pm), nearby in Plaza del Conde. In this work of great spiritual intensity, the body of Gonzalo Ruíz de Toledo is being

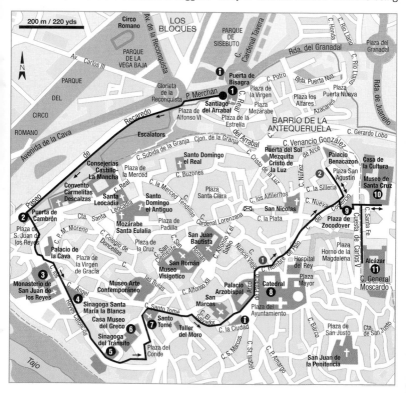

Madonna and Child

The Cathedral's Spanish Gothic façade

carried by the saints Stephen and Augustine. He is buried in this church.

CATEDRAL

Follow the signs to the exquisite **Catedral** ❽ (www.catedralprimada.es; Mon–Sat 10am–6pm, Sun 2pm–6pm). Begun in 1226, it was completed in 1493. Although primarily a superb example of Spanish Gothic, it also has Mudéjar Baroque and neoclassical elements. It contains some superb paintings by El Greco, Titian, Van Dyck and Goya. Look out for the intricately-carved walnut choir stalls.

PLAZA DE ZOCODOVER

From the cathedral, turn right up calle Hombre de Palo, where **Adolfo** restaurant, see ❶, is a smart place for lunch. You emerge at the triangular **Plaza de Zocodover** ❾, laid out in the late-16th century on the site of the Moorish cattle market. It was the scene of medieval jousting tournaments and bullfights, as well as executions by the Inquisition.

Through the arch off the square is the **Museo de Santa Cruz** ❿ (Mon–Sat 10am–7pm, Sun 10am–2pm), a Renaissance orphanage and hospital housing paintings by El Greco and Goya.

ALCÁZAR

It is a few minutes' walk up the hill to the imposing **Alcázar** ⓫, the highest point in the city. Built in the 16th century, it has a Plateresque portal by Alonso de Covarrubias, while Juan de Herrera designed the south façade. A Nationalist stronghold in the Civil War, it was relentlessly attacked by the Republicans. Today it is home to the **Museo del Ejército** (Army Museum; www.museo.ejercito. es; Mon–Tue, Thu–Sun 10am–5pm), charting Spain's military history.

From the Plaza de Zocodover, head down calle Sillería to the **Mercado de San Agustín**, see ❷, where you can end this route with a drink and bite to eat.

Food and Drink

❶ ADOLFO

Calle Hombre de Palo 7; tel: 925 227321; www.adolforestaurante.com; Mon–Sun 1–4pm, 8pm–midnight; €€
Adolfo Muñoz was pioneering local produce and updating traditional dishes in this medieval building long before it became fashionable to do so. Order the red partridge to savour what Toledan cuisine is all about.

❷ MERCADO DE SAN AGUSTÍN

Calle de la Cuesta del Aguila 1 y 3; tel: 696104308; www.mercadodesanagustin. com; Mon–Sun 10am–1.30am, Fri–Sat until 2am; €
You can have anything from a craft beer to a venison burger at this gourmet food court. At dusk, locals gather for cocktails at the rooftop bar to gaze across the beautiful skyline.

The austere lines of El Escorial

EL ESCORIAL AND VALLE DE LOS CAÍDOS

Built by Felipe II in the 16th century, El Escorial makes a powerful statement about the power of the Habsburg dynasty. The vast granite structure contains a wealth of artworks, including paintings by El Greco, Titian and Rubens.

DISTANCE: 54km (33 miles)
TIME: A full day
START/END: El Escorial
POINTS TO NOTE: Take bus 661 or 664 from the Intercambiador de Moncloa, or the C3 train from Atocha, Sol, Nuevos Ministerios or Chamartín stations (both take about an hour). For the Valle de los Caídos, the 660 bus leaves San Lorenzo de El Escorial at 3.15pm and returns at 5.30pm.

Allow a whole morning to visit the monastery. You could then have lunch before catching the bus to the Valle de los Caídos. San Lorenzo de El Escorial is a pleasant town in its own right and it is worth seeing the monastery from the outside even if you do not have time to go inside.

REAL MONASTERIO DE SAN LORENZO DE EL ESCORIAL

The **Real Monasterio de San Lorenzo de El Escorial ❶** (Royal Monastery of San Lorenzo de El Escorial; www.patri-monionacional.es/real-sitio/real-sitio-de-san-lorenzo-de-el-escorial; Tue–Sun Oct–Mar 10am–6pm, Apr–Sept 10am–7pm; free last three hours Wed and Thu) is a solemn structure that reflects Felipe II's austere nature and the strength of his religious devotion. It is said that the king decided that this was the perfect site on 10 August, 1577, which is Saint Lawrence's day and also the date of Spain's victory over France at St Quentin. To commemorate this, the monastery is named after the saint and the parallelogram plan is said to represent the gridiron on which he was burnt to death.

The building measures 205 metres (672 ft) from north to south and 160 metres (525 ft) from east to west, with more than 2,600 windows and 1,200 doors. Although most of the original art collection is in the Prado museum, there are many masterpieces on display, including works by Veronese, Tintoretto, El Greco, Ribera, Rubens, Martin de Vos and Michiel van Coxcie.

In the king's spartan chamber, the bed was positioned so that he could see the high altar of the church and

The exquisite Biblioteca Real at El Escorial

also the surrounding countryside. Also part of the complex are the office from which he boasted he ruled the world from two inches of paper and the octagonal marble **Panteón de los Reyes**, containing the remains of nearly all the Spanish monarchs.

The magnificent **Basílica** is crowned by a dome with a diameter of 92 metres (302 ft) set on a drum with frescoes by Luca Giordano. The **Capilla Mayor** is the spiritual powerhouse of the monastery and features a marble and gilded bronze retable flanked on either side by sculptural groups by Leone Leoni of Carlos V with his family and Felipe II with three of his wives.

The barrel-vaulted library, the **Biblioteca Real**, is 55 metres (180 ft) long with a marble floor and ceiling frescoes by Tibaldi. The shelves contain more than 40,000 documents and books, arranged with the leaves facing outwards to aid conservation by allowing air to permeate the paper.

During the reign of Carlos III in the 18th century, Juan de Villanueva designed two lodges near the monastery for recreational purposes. The **Casita del Príncipe** ❷ (also known as the Casa de Abajo) is situated in the Jardínes del Príncipe down the hill to the east. The **Casita del Infante** ❸ (or Casita de Arriba), about 2km (1.2

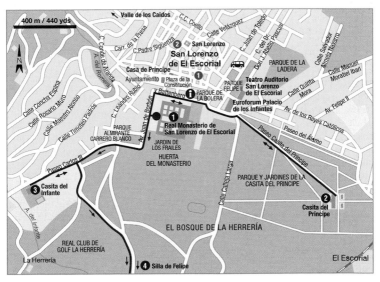

Valle de los Caídos marks the site of a basilica and monastery

miles) along the Paseo de Carlos III, is a hunting pavilion that was home to Juan Carlos I, the former king, when he was a student. About 5km (3 miles) away, in the hills to the south, is the **Silla de Felipe** ❹ (Philip's Seat), where the king used to sit in a chair carved out of the rocks to watch his dream being realised.

Ever since the railway was built in the 19th century, Madrilenians have flocked to **San Lorenzo de El Escorial** at weekends to enjoy the fresh air and cooler temperatures. Cultural events and festivals throughout the summer mean there is always a lively atmosphere. The town has an elegant 18th-century theatre, the **Coliseo Real** and some attractive bars and restaurants, including the traditional **La Cueva**, see ❶ and the more creative **Montia**, see ❷.

VALLE DE LOS CAÍDOS

The **Valle de los Caídos** (Valley of the Fallen; valledeloscaidos.es; Tue–Sun Oct–Mar 10am–7pm, Apr–Sept 10am–7pm) is the site of a basilica and monastery, marked by a cross that is visible from a great distance. Made of local granite, it is nearly 150 metres high (492 ft) with a span of 46 metres (151 ft).

Construction of the monument begun in the 1940s on the orders of General Franco, supposedly to commemorate those who died in Spain's Civil War (1936–39). After the war ended, Republican prisoners, many of whom died in the process, were drafted in to dig the site out of the rocky mountainside. Completed nearly two decades later in 1958, the basilica contains an enormous crypt that houses the tombs of General Franco and José Antonio Primo de Rivera, the founder of the far-right Falangist party. More than 30,000 soldiers, both Nationalist and Republican, are believed to be buried in the walls of the basilica and in the hillside around it. Campaigns have been underway for years to move Franco's tomb, exhume the victims of the war and create a museum to offer a more balanced view of the conflict.

Food and Drink

❶ LA CUEVA

Calle San Antón 4; tel: 91 8901516; www.mesonlacueva.com; Tue–Sun 1–4pm, 9–11pm, Sun lunch only; €€
In a building dating back to the 18th century, La Cueva serves traditional Castilian dishes with tasty stews and meat roasted in a charcoal oven.

❷ MONTIA

Calle Calvario 4; tel: 91 1336988; www.montia.es; Wed–Sun 1.30–3.30pm, 8.30–10.30pm, Wed and Sun lunch only; €€€
Five minutes' walk from the monastery, Montia serves contemporary cuisine with a constantly changing menu of dishes created from the best local produce available. Book ahead.

Segovia's skyline

SEGOVIA

Set on a ridge in the Castilian countryside, Segovia is a delightful town of honey-coloured buildings and Romanesque churches, where the rich heritage mixes with a lively contemporary cultural scene. Spend the morning sightseeing before a lunch of suckling pig or roast lamb.

DISTANCE: 88km (55 miles)
TIME: A full day
START: Acueducto
END: Alcázar
POINTS TO NOTE: The train to Segovia from Chamartín station takes 30 minutes. La Sepúlvedana runs a frequent bus service from the Intercambiador de Moncloa, which takes an hour. It is usually always cooler in Segovia than Madrid, so take an extra layer.

Long before Madrid became the capital of Spain in the 16th century, Segovia was one of the most important cities in Spain, as borne out by the many Romanesque churches that you come across almost at every turn as you wander around. The promontory, shaped like a teardrop, is a dense mesh of ochre buildings with spindly spires seeming to jostle for prime spots on the skyline.

While the old town has Unesco World Heritage status, there is nothing staid about Segovia. Lots of palaces, churches and monasteries are now used for exhibitions, concerts and other creative activities. There are characterful shops too and many Madrilenians come here at weekends just for a roast lunch at one of the traditional restaurants.

ACUEDUCTO

Segovia's best-known landmark, the **Acueducto ❶**, was built 2,000 years by the Romans and carried the city's water supply until half a century ago. Great slabs of granite from the Guadarrama mountains form 118 arches that stretch across the Plaza del Azoguejo and beyond for 813 metres/yds. It is astonishing to think that there is no cement holding the structure together.

The aquaduct stands in the **Plaza del Azoguejo**, where there is a tourist information centre. Also here is the **Mesón de Cándido**, see ❶, Segovia's most famous restaurant. From the square, calle Cervantes, flanked by shops and restaurants, leads up the hill through the centre of the town. On the right is the **Casa de los Picos**, with a 16th-century façade of pointed granite stones.

Some of the Acueducto's 118 arches

The street changes its name to calle Juan Bravo, who was the leader of the uprising in the 16th century when the local inhabitants rebelled against Carlos V and the nobility. There is a statue of him in the **Plaza de San Martín ②**, where the 12th-century **Iglesia de San Martín** has a Mudéjar tower. At the top of the steps on the right of the square is the 15th-century **Torreón de Lozoya**, a tower that is part of a palace.

PLAZA MAYOR

Continuing up the street, you emerge in the splendid, porticoed **Plaza Mayor ③**,

with the 17th-century town hall facing you and several attractive cafés and restaurants with terraces to choose from. The **Mesón José María**, see ②, one of the best traditional places to eat, is just off the square.

Catedral

On the left of the square is the late-Gothic **Catedral ④** (Mon–Sun Nov–Mar 9.30am–7pm, Apr–Oct 9am–9.30pm; free Sun 9am–11am). Designed by Juan Gil de Hontañón and his son Rodrigo, the dainty structure with filigree spires was built in the 16th century. The elegant interior, softened by golden sandstone,

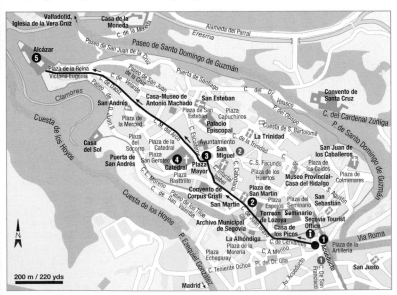

The dainty Cathedral

The hills around Segovia

features stained-glass windows made by Flemish and Spanish craftsmen.

ALCÁZAR

Continuing past the cathedral, you reach the **Alcázar** ❺ (www.alcazardesegovia. com; Mon–Sun Nov–Mar 10am–6pm, Apr–Oct 10am–8pm). The fairy-tale castle with slate turrets, which looks more Bavarian than Castilian, stands at the end of the limestone ridge at the point where the Eresma and Clamores rivers meet. Although there had been a fortress here since the 13th century, this structure was built in the second half of the 19th century after a fire. Weapons and suits of armour are on display in the museum and there are panoramic views of the town and the surrounding countryside from the tower.

Suits of armour in the Alcázar

Food and Drink

❶ MESÓN DE CÁNDIDO

Plaza del Azoguejo 5; 921 425911; www.mesondecandido.es; Mon–Sun 1–4.30pm, 8–11pm; €€
With a history going back more than a century, Cándido is deservedly renowned throughout Spain and beyond for its roast suckling pig and lamb, as well as other regional specialities. Right by the aqueduct in an historic building, eating here is the quintessential Segovia experience.

❷ MESÓN JOSÉ MARÍA

Calle Cronista Lecea 11; tel: 921 461111; www.restaurantejosemaria. com; Mon–Thu 9am–1am, Fri 9am–2am; Sat 10am–2am, Sun 10am–1am; €€
Just off the Plaza Mayor, José María serves superb roasts and more elaborate dishes too. If you don't want a full meal, call in for a glass of wine in the lively bar at the front of the restaurant, where you get a free tapa with every drink.

DIRECTORY

Hand-picked hotels and restaurants to suit all budgets and tastes, organised by area, plus select nightlife listings, an alphabetical listing of practical information, a language guide and an overview of the best books and films to give you a flavour of the city.

View across Madrid from the Principal

ACCOMMODATION

Madrid has an excellent range of accommodation, whether you are looking for a luxury hotel or a no-frills base. Many hotels, even when part of major chains, occupy elegant late-19th-century buildings, with several in former palaces.

There has been a boom in recent years of stylish, inexpensive places, which usually offer pared-back rooms with good beds and showers, while not bothering with facilities that many people on a city break simply do not need.

At the top end of the market, meanwhile, there are some stunning new properties with cutting-edge design, Michelin-starred restaurants, sumptuous spas and spectacular rooftop bars.

There has been a huge growth in the holiday apartment market in the last decade – a great option for those travelling with children.

As the centre of Madrid is quite compact, you can usually walk from your hotel to most places you are likely to want to go in less than 20 minutes. Plaza de Santa Ana, Chueca and Plaza de España are good areas to base yourself. Some of the smartest hotels are in the Salamanca district, near good shops and with plenty of restaurants nearby. You might need to take a short metro or taxi ride to get to some of the museums and other sights, but there is a less touristy atmosphere than around the Puerta del Sol.

There are often bargains to be had in August, when many locals go on holiday, particularly at high-end hotels. January and February are the cheapest months.

Puerta del Sol and the Gran Vía

Círculo Gran Vía Autograph Collection

Gran Vía 24; tel: 91 5210300; https://autograph-hotels.marriott.com/hotel/hotel-circulo-gran-via; €€€€

This adults-only luxury hotel occupies an ornate 1920s building on the Gran Vía. The 71 rooms in mid-century modern style are spacious and stylish and there is a gym and a roof terrace.

Dear Hotel

Gran Vía 80; tel: 91 4123200; www.dearhotelmadrid.com; €€

It is all about the views at the four-star Dear, where there are a lot of luxe touches in the 162 Scandi-style rooms. The best vistas are from the rooftop bar and restaurant, where there is also a plunge pool.

> Price guide for a double room for one night without breakfast:
> €€€€ = more than 250 euros
> €€€ = 150–250 euros
> €€ = 80–150 euros
> € = less than 80 euros

A luxury room at the Principal

Emperador

Gran Vía 53; tel: 91 5472800;
www.emperadorhotel.com; €€€
The rooftop pool at the four-star Emperador is a haven on hot summer days. The hotel, opened in 1947, exudes traditional glamour with 232 classically-designed rooms. Some have terraces and there are spectacular views from the upper floors.

Iberostar De Las Letras

Gran Vía 11; tel: 91 5237980;
www.hoteldelasletras.com; €€
There is a bookish theme here, with literary quotes behind the beds in the 109 rooms, which have high ceilings and large windows. Some have balconies and there is a suite on two levels in the tower on the corner.

Indigo

Calle Silva 6; tel: 91 2008585;
www.indigomadrid.com; €€
The four-star Indigo has 85 rooms in opulent jewel shades with luxurious beds. With a bar and a pool up on the roof, it is a cool place to hang out in summer.

NH Suecia

Calle Marqués de Casa Riera 4; tel: 91 2000570; www.nh-collection.com/hotel/nh-collection-madrid-suecia; €€€
A favourite of Ernest Hemingway and Che Guevara, with 123 rooms and suites on 10 floors. Revamped in 2016 by star designer Lázaro Rosa-Violán. Guests sip cocktails in the decadent Hemingway bar or up on the roof terrace.

Praktik Metropol

Calle Montera 47; tel: 91 5212935;
www.praktikmetropol.com; €
This industrial-style hotel has a welcoming atmosphere with a pleasant lounge and basic but comfortable rooms.

Principal

Calle Marqués de Valdeiglesias 1, corner Gran Vía 2; tel: 91 5218743;
www.theprincipalmadridhotel.com; €€€€
This five-star hotel set in a grand early-20th century building has 76 rooms and a calming grey colour scheme. The restaurant is overseen by Michelin-starred chef Ramon Freixa and there are two chic roof terraces for cocktails.

Vincci 66

Gran Vía 66; tel: 91 5504299; www.vincci hoteles.com/eng/Hotels/Spain/Madrid/Vincci-Via-66; €€
This 1940s building has stunning features, such as a marble staircase and stained-glass windows. The 116 rooms are decorated with luxurious fabrics in crimson and gold and there are fabulous views form the 10th-floor roof terrace.

Vincci The Mint

Gran Vía 10; tel: 91 2030650;
http://en.vinccithemint.com; €€€
With zingy design in shades of green, the four-star, fashionable hotel occupies an elegant, early 20th-century building and has a rooftop bar with spectacular views. The 88 rooms and suites are spacious and light.

A vast suite at Gran Meliá Palacio de los Duques

Plaza Mayor and Madrid de Los Austrias

La Posada del Dragón
Calle Cava Baja 14; tel: 91 1191424; www.posadadeldragon.com; €€
In the oldest and most atmospheric part of Madrid on a street lined with tapas bars, this chic three-star hotel with 27 rooms blends contemporary style with traditional architecture.

Mayerling
Calle del Conde de Romanones 6; tel: 91 4201580; www.mayerlinghotel.com; €€
The two-star has 22 rooms in a former fabric warehouse in a handy location. With contemporary design and a sun terrace, it is a pleasant no-frills option.

Petit Palace Posada del Peine
Calle Postas 17; tel: 91 5238151; www.petitpalaceposadadelpeine.com; €€
In a characterful historic building alongside the Plaza Mayor, this four-star hotel is good for families as some of the contemporary rooms have bunks as well as double beds.

Posada del León de Oro
Calle Cava Baja 12; tel: 91 1191494; www.posadadelleondeoro.com; €€
A coaching inn set around a courtyard is now a characterful four-star boutique hotel with 17 romantic rooms. Good restaurant and a popular wine bar.

The Hat
Calle Imperial 9; tel: 91 7728572; www.thehatmadrid.com; €
This is a hostel with the style of a boutique hotel. Fuelled by biomass energy, with distressed wood and leather furniture in the lobby bar and a groovy roof terrace, it has double and family rooms as well as dorms.

Royal Madrid

Central Palace Madrid
Plaza de Oriente 2; tel: 91 5482018; www.centralpalacemadrid.com; €€
Although lacking facilities, this quirky place has quite possibly the best location in the city, opposite the Palacio Real. On the upper floors of an elegant building, it has attractive rooms in natural tones.

Gala
Costanilla de los Angeles 15; tel: 91 5419692; www.hostalgala.com; €
On the second floor (with a lift) of a 19th-century building within easy walking distance of shops and sights, the no-frills Gala has 22 rooms, some suitable for families, with a modern design.

Gran Meliá Palacio de los Duques
Cuesta de Santo Domingo 5; tel: 91 5416700; www.melia.com/en/hotels/spain/madrid/gran-melia-palacio-de-los-duques; €€€€
This five-star hotel with 180 rooms and suites in a lavishly remodelled palace near the Teatro Real is among the best in Madrid with superb service, outstanding food and a rooftop pool. Inside there is a Velázquez theme, inspired by the tones of his palette.

The loft–style lobby at Only You Atocha

Room Mate Laura

Travesía de Trujillo 3; tel: 91 011670; https://room-matehotels.com/en/laura; €€

This chic three-star hotel is hidden away from the crowds by the Descalzas Reales convent. Designer Tomás Alia has put large prints of Juana de Austria, the founder of the convent, in prime position in the loft-style rooms, some of which have kitchens and are great for families.

Room Mate Mario

Calle Campomanes 4; tel: 91 5488548; https://room-matehotels.com/en/mario; €€

On a quiet street near the Teatro Real and the Royal Palace, this is a smart yet inexpensive option that appeals to design fans with splashes of colour zinging up the white décor in the 54 rooms.

Room007 Select Sol

Calle de las Fuentes 13; tel: 91 4496181 www.room007.com/madrid/sol; €

With good beds and crisp contemporary design, this is a basic but attractive place to stay in a central location. Facilities include kitchen and free WiFi.

Toc

Plaza Celenque 3-5; tel: 91 5321304; www.tochostels.com/madrid; €€

If you want to stay somewhere comfortable, fun and reasonably-priced in the centre of Madrid, this stylish hostel in a handsome building fits the bill. There are double and family rooms as well as dorms, and facilities including a kitchen.

The Paseo del Prado and the Retiro Park

Doubletree by Hilton Madrid Prado

Calle San Agustín 3; tel: 91 3600820; www.dtbhmadridprado.com; €€€€

This four-star has a five-star boutique feel and is a favourite of art and fashion folk. Close to the Prado and tapas bars, it has 61 rooms in grey and indigo tones. The Kirei Japanese restaurant is excellent.

Only You Atocha

Paseo de la Infanta Isabel 13; tel: 91 4097876; www.onlyyouhotels.com/en/hotels/only-you-hotel-atocha; €€€

With a big wow factor owing to the dazzling loft-style design by Lázaro Rosa-Violán, this four-star hotel between the Retiro Park and Atocha train station has 205 rooms and suites on seven floors with lots of natural light.

Palacio del Retiro Autograph Collection

Calle Alfonso XII 14; tel: 91 5237460; https://autograph-hotels.marriott.com/hotel/hotel-palacio-del-retiro; €€€€

Original features contrast with contemporary design in this early-20th-century palace, now a five-star luxury hotel. The 50 rooms and suites all have a view of the Retiro park opposite. A grand staircase and stained-glass windows add to the grandeur.

Petit Palace Savoy Alfonso XII

Calle Alfonso XII 18; tel: 91 522 1920; http://en.petitpalacesavoyalfonsoxii.com; €€

Traditional room décor at the Ritz

Shades of mauve and grey create a soothing vibe in this dainty 19th-century palace, situated on one of the smartest corners in the city. Bikes available.

Ritz Madrid

Plaza de la Lealtad 5; tel: 91 7016767; www.mandarinoriental.com/madrid/hotel-ritz/luxury-hotel; €€€€
Classic luxury and exquisite service make the Ritz one of Madrid's top hotels. Some rooms have chandeliers and silk canopies over the beds and most are furnished with antiques. The terrace is a delightful spot for drinks or brunch, even if you are not staying in the hotel.

Sleep'n Atocha

Calle Dr. Drumen 4; tel: 91 5399807; www.sleepnatocha.com; €€
Opposite both the Reina Sofía museum and Atocha station, this unfussy stylish hotel has comfortable rooms, some with balconies.

Villa Real

Plaza de las Cortes 10; tel: 91 4203767; www.hotelvillareal.com; €€€
Close to the major museums, the five-star Villa Real is a classic hotel that is filled with extraordinary artworks – antiquities include Syrian mosaics and Greek vases. There are 115 rooms and suites, some duplex and most with small balconies.

Wellington

Calle Velázquez 8; tel: 91 5754400; www.hotel-wellington.com; €€€

The five-star Wellington is one of Madrid's most renowned hotels, with a pool and garden on the rooftop, a luxury spa and sumptuous rooms with marble bathrooms. The Kabuki restaurant has a Michelin star and the Goizeko offers superb Basque cuisine.

Westin Palace

Plaza de las Cortes 7; tel: 91 360 8000; www.westinpalacemadrid.com; €€€€
Wallow in five-star glamour at one of Madrid's most renowned historic hotels. The 467 spacious rooms have deep carpets and sumptuous beds.

Plaza de Santa Ana, the Barrio de las Letras and Lavapiés

Artrip

Calle Valencia 11; tel: 91 539 3282; www.artriphotel.com; €€
In multicultural Lavapiés, near the Reina Sofía museum and Atocha train station, this is a 17-room, friendly, no-frills hotel with contemporary design in a traditional building.

Casual Madrid del Teatro

Calle Echegaray 1; tel: 91 429 9551; www.casualhoteles.com/en/hotels-madrid/casual-del-teatro; €
The 37 rooms at this fun, no-frills option are themed to recreate the sets of musicals and plays. In a handy location, it offers good facilities for families.

Me Madrid Reina Victoria

Plaza de Santa Ana, 14; tel: 91 701 6000;

Urban's inviting rooftop pool

www.mebymelia.com/hotels/me-madrid;
€€€

This four-star, buzzy hotel in an historic building in an excellent location is a really fun place to stay with a great restaurant and rooftop bar. The 192 rooms and suites have purple fridges and hangover kits.

NH Collection Palacio de Tepa

Calle San Sebastián 2; tel: 91 6008146;
www.nh-collection.com/hotel/nh-collection-madrid-palacio-de-tepa; €€€

This elegant five-star hotel occupies a palatial neoclassical building designed by Juan de Villanueva, the architect of the Prado museum. Some rooms have vaulted or sloping wooden ceilings and there are duplex spaces that are good for families.

OK Hostel

Calle Juanelo 24; tel: 91 4293744;
www.okhostels.com; €

Smart design, a warm vibe and a location in a less touristy, more traditional part of the centre combine to make the OK one of the best hostels in the city. Double rooms and dorms available.

Pasaje

Calle del Pozo 4; tel: 91 5212995;
www.elpasajehs.com; €€

In a characterful building on a pedestrianised lane, the three-star Pasaje has 14 rooms which are a bit basic but have all the facilities are you likely to need on a short stay.

Room Mate Alicia

Calle del Prado 2; tel: 91 3896095;
https://room-matehotels.com/en/alicia; €€

Top interior designer Pascua Ortega transformed a 20th-century industrial building into a light-filled space, which is now a favourite with fashion and media types. Pale wood contrasts with bold splashes of colour in the 34 rooms. Two splendid duplex suites have roof terraces and plunge pools.

Urban

Carretera de San Jerónimo 34; tel: 91 7877770; www.hotelurban.com; €€€€

This five-star is a fashionable design hotel filled with ancient Egyptian, African and Oriental artefacts and contemporary artworks. A rooftop pool and the Cebo restaurant, one of the best in Madrid, add to the allure.

Vincci Soho

Calle del Prado 18; tel: 91 1414100;
http://en.vinccisoho.com; €€€

Purple, pink and red tones perk up the interiors of the five 19th-century buildings occupied by this four-star hotel in the heart of the Barrio de Las Letras. Lavish room décor and relaxing courtyard.

Chueca, Malasaña and Conde Duque

B&B Fuencarral 52

Calle Fuencarral 52; tel: 91 2787962;
www.hotel-bb.es/en/hotel/madrid-fuencarral-52; €€

This restored traditional building is a handy place to stay if you are planning on spending time in the fashionable Chueca and Malasaña areas. Rooms are fresh, bright and modern and there is a roof terrace with a vertical garden.

Eurostars Central

Mejía Lequerica 10; tel: 91 3967180; www.eurostarshotels.com/eurostars-central.html; €€

Contemporary, minimalist design, combined with large rooms and a trendy rather than touristy location make this four-star hotel a good choice. The 135 rooms and suites all face outwards and those on the top floor have terraces.

Only You Boutique

Calle Barquillo 21; tel: 91 0052222; www.onlyyouhotels.com/en/hotels/only-you-boutique-hotel-madrid; €€€€

The street-level bar and restaurant are popular places to meet at this chic boutique hotel in a former palatial residence remodelled by designer Lázaro Rosa-Violán. Rooms have a navy and white colour scheme and the best have spectacular terraces and are more like apartments.

Room Mate Óscar

Plaza Pedro Zerolo 12; tel: 91 7011173; https://.room-matehotels.com/en/oscar; €€

A fashionable and comfortable place to stay in the heart of Chueca with 74 rooms in a Bauhaus-style building with peppy design by Tomás Alia, a rooftop pool and a lively vibe.

Urso

Calle Mejía Lequerica 8; tel: 91 444 4458; www.hotelurso.com; €€€

This discreet, five-star boutique hotel is opposite the Barceló market. The palatial building retains many original features, including stained-glass windows. There is an excellent restaurant and a spa with a small pool.

Plaza de España and Moncloa

Barceló Torre de Madrid

Plaza de España 18; tel: 91 5242399; https:/hotelbarcelotorredemadrid.com; €€€€

Top Spanish designer Jaime Hayón has created fresh interiors in jewel and berry shades at this five-star hotel with 258 rooms in the Torre de Madrid skyscraper. It has a great cocktail bar, a spa and an indoor pool.

Casón del Tormes

Calle del Río 7; tel: 91 541 9746; www.hotelcasondeltormes.com; €€

The three-star Casón del Tormes has a family feel and a handy location. The 63 rooms are decorated in classic style and rates are usually reasonable for the standard.

Exe Moncloa

Calle Arcipreste de Hita 10; tel: 91 745 9299; www.hotelexemoncloa.com; €€

There is a lively vibe at this four-star hotel in buzzy Moncloa. With a cool roof terrace, easy access to public transport and affordable rates, it is an attractive option in a less touristy area.

Meliá Madrid Princesa

Calle Princesa 27; tel: 91 5418200;
www1.melia.com/en/hotels/spain/madrid/
melia-madrid-princesa; €€€

This well-established five-star hotel has 269 comfortable, modern rooms, superb service and a convenient location. It suits frequent travellers who need a hotel with guaranteed standards throughout.

Paseo de la Castellana and Salamanca

AC Recoletos

Calle Recoletos 18; tel: 91 4361382;
www.marriott.com/hotels/travel/madrc-ac-
hotel-recoletos; €€€

This four-star hotel, originally a grand private residence, combines neoclassical style with minimalist chic interiors. On a quiet street near the shops on calle Serrano, the Retiro park, the Plaza de Cibeles and the airport bus stop, it is a convenient, comfortable base.

Barceló Emperatriz

Calle López de Hoyos 4; tel: 91 3422490;
www.barceloemperatriz.com; €€€€

This ultra-stylish five-star hotel is inspired by Eugenia de Montijo, the 19th-century Empress who was married Napoleon III. It feels grand and palatial but in a contemporary rather than a stuffy way. The 146 rooms have beautiful bathrooms and there is a small pool on the roof terrace.

Hesperia Madrid

Paseo de la Castellana 57; tel: 91 2108800;
www.hesperia-madrid.com; €€€

This five-star hotel was revamped by Pascua Ortega, one of Spain's most well-known interior designers. The 171 rooms and suites combine traditional style with Art Deco features and contemporary touches. The Santceloni restaurant has two Michelin stars.

NH Collection Colón

Calle Marqués de Zurgena 4; tel: 91 5750800; www.nh-collection.com/es/hotel/
nh-collection-madrid-colon; €€€

Designed in the mid-20th century by renowned architect Luis Gutiérrez-Soto, the four-star hotel was totally remodelled in 2016. It has 146 rooms and suites, an outdoor pool, a good gym and a handy location by the best shopping streets.

Tótem

Calle Hermosilla 23; tel: 91 4260035;
www.totem-madrid.com; €€€

Occupying one of the most prestigious corners in the city, the four-star Tótem has 67 rooms in contemporary style in tones of grey and blue. It feels like a private club and there is a stylish bar and restaurant.

Único

Calle Claudio Coello 67; tel: 91 7810173;
www.unicohotelmadrid.com; €€€€

This five-star hotel has 44 rooms and suites and occupies an elegant 19th-century palace on one of Madrid's most exclusive streets. Its Ramon Freixa restaurant has two Michelin stars.

The family-run La Casa del Abuelo tapas bar

RESTAURANTS

The streets of Madrid are packed with places to eat and drink, ranging from basic bars to elegant Michelin-starred restaurants. Walking around the city, you come across stylish cafés, boisterous tapas bars, chic gastrobars, classic Castilian restaurants and more informal brasseries with contemporary design.

Lots of locals eat out every day and most Madrilenians pop into their neighbourhood bar for a coffee, a beer, a snack and a chat at some point in the day.

The usual restaurant opening hours are 1pm to 4pm for lunch and 9pm until midnight for dinner, although these times are becoming increasingly flexible. Madrilenians tend to arrive at a restaurant between 2pm and 3pm for lunch, while 10pm is the key booking time for dinner, so it is much easier to get a table without a reservation if you pitch up an hour earlier than those key times. For anywhere except very high end or fashionable restaurants, you do not usually have to book more than a day or two in advance. Friday and Saturday nights are the by far the busiest, while Sunday evenings and all day Monday are

when places are most likely to be closed. A lot of restaurants close for at least two weeks in August.

Tapas bars keep similar hours for lunch, but get going earlier in the evening, from around 8pm. Cafés are open all day.

Puerta del Sol and the Gran Vía

La Casa del Abuelo
Calle Victoria 12; tel: 91 0000133; www.lacasadelabuelo.es; Mon–Sun noon–midnight, Fri–Sat until 1am; €
This frantically busy family-run bar is an essential stop for a vermouth or a beer with a dish of prawns sizzling away in olive oil pepped up with garlic and chili.

Lhardy
Carrera de San Jerónimo 8; tel: 91 5213385; https://lhardy.com; Mon–Sun 1–3.30pm, 8.30–11pm, Sun lunch only; €€€
You may well spot a politician, actor or writer at Lhardy, which opened in 1839. You can have a drink in the shop, where ornate cabinets display dainty sandwiches, or eat in one of the grand dining rooms. Their *cocido* stew is renowned.

La Tasquita de Enfrente
Calle Ballesta 6; tel: 91 5325449; www.latasquitadeenfrente.com; Mon–Sat 2–5.30pm, 8pm–midnight; €€€€
Book ahead at Juanjo López Bedmar's tiny restaurant in the Triball area, which

Price guide based on a two-course meal with one glass of wine:
€€€€ = more than 60 euros
€€€ = 40–60 euros
€€ = 25–40 euros
€ = less than 25 euros

Dining at Los Galayos on Plaza Mayor

is one of the best in town and a favourite of foodies and off-duty chefs. The ultra seasonal tasting menu features the best of Spanish produce.

La Terraza del Casino

Calle Alcalá 15; tel: 91 5218700; www.casinodemadrid.es; Tue–Sat 1.30–3.30pm, 9–11pm; €€€€

Paco Roncero's flagship restaurant has two Michelin stars and occupies an impressive space at the top of the Casino de Madrid private club. Expect to be surprised by every dish. With a romantic terrace, this is a spot for a special occasion.

Plaza Mayor and Madrid de Los Austrias

Botín

Calle Cuchilleros 17; tel: 91 3664217; www.botin.es; Mon–Sun 1–4pm, 8pm–midnight; €€€

Founded in 1725, Botín is officially the oldest restaurant in the world and was a favourite of Ernest Hemingway. The roast suckling pig or lamb are the dishes to devour in one of the tiled dining rooms or in the vaulted cellar.

Casa Revuelta

Calle Latoneros 3; tel: 91 3663332; Tue–Sun 10.30am–4pm, 7–11pm, Sun lunch only; €

Founded in the 1960s, Casa Revuelta is one of the most traditional taverns in Madrid. People come here just for the tortilla potato omelette, but the cod strips in batter and the meatballs in tomato sauce are legendary too.

La Musa

Costanilla de San Andrés 12, Plaza de la Paja; tel: 91 3540255; www.grupolamusa.com; Mon–Sun 10am–1am, Fri–Sat until 2am; €

With tables in the square and a buzzy vibe inside, La Musa is always busy. The menu has something to suit everyone, with a mix of Mediterranean and Asian dishes to share.

Los Galayos

Calle Botoneras 5; tel: 91 3663028; www.losgalayos.net; Mon–Sun noon–midnight; €€

With a terrace on the Plaza Mayor and a brick-vaulted dining room, Los Galayos is as traditional as it gets. Open since 1894, come here for Madrilenian dishes such as suckling pig and *cocido* stew. Or just have tapas at the 17th-century wooden bar.

Taberna Los Huevos de Lucio

Calle Cava Baja 30; tel: 91 3662984; Mon–Sun 1–4pm, 8.30pm–midnight; €€

Run by the younger generation of the family behind revered restaurant Casa Lucio across the street, the signature dish at this more informal tavern is *huevos rotos* – fried eggs broken over a pile of chips with ham or *pisto* (similar to ratatouille). Sit at the bar or book a table in the attractive dining room at the back.

Royal Madrid

De María

Plaza de Isabel II 8; tel: 91 5479305;

Superb presentation at Cebo

www.demariarestaurante.es; Mon–Sun
12.30–4.30pm, 8.30pm–12.30am; €€
Specialises in Argentinian grilled meat
dishes. As well as excellent steaks, the
menu includes pasta and salads. Friendly
staff. Several branches around the city.

El Anciano Rey de los Vinos

Calle Bailén 19; tel: 91 559 5332;
www.elancianoreydelosvinos.es; Mon,
Wed–Sun 9am–midnight; €
This traditional tavern with outdoor
tables has been open for more than a
century. Opposite the Almudena cathedral and close to the Royal Palace, it is a
handy spot for a drink – try their own-la-
bel wine or draught vermouth – or a sit-
down meal.

La Taberna El Mollete

Calle La Bola 4; tel: 91 5477820;
www.tabernaelmollete.com; Mon–Sat
10am–5pm, 8pm–1am; €
There are just a handful of tables with
red and white checked cloths on an
upper level above the bar at El Mollete.
Everything appeals on the short menu,
particularly the avocado salad, gorgon-
zola *croquetas* and *ibérico* pork.

Palo Cortado

Calle Unión 5; tel: 91 5472500;
www.tabernapalocortado.com; Tue–Sat
1–4pm, 9pm–midnight; €€
A pretty bar and restaurant in the Ópera
area that specialises in sherry. Dishes
include marinated dogfish in Oloroso
sherry sauce.

The Paseo del Prado and the Retiro Park

Bumpgreen

Calle Velázquez 11; tel: 91 1962018;
www.bumpgreen.com; Mon–Fri 9am–
midnight, Sat 10am–midnight, Sun
10am–6pm; €
Open-brick walls and a vertical garden
set the scene at Bumpgreen, which specialises in organic produce and offers
quinoa porridge for breakfast and a
wide range of salads as well as fish and
meat dishes, juices and cocktails.

El Brilliante

Plaza del Emperador Carlos V; tel: 91
5286966; www.barelbrillante.es; Mon–Sun
7am–12.30am; €
Before or after the Reina Sofía museum,
pop into this most typical of Madrid bars
for a beer or two and their famous *bocadillo de calamares*, a long roll stuffed
with fried squid rings, or tuck into the
meatballs or grilled prawns.

El Perro y La Galleta

Calle Claudio Coello 1; tel: 606 822421;
www.elperroygalleta.com; Tue–Sun 10am–
12.30am, 1.30am at weekends; €€
Dogs feature prominently in the décor
at this smart bistro-style café by the
park. A varied menu of modern Spanish dishes includes plenty of choices for
vegetarians. It is good for breakfast too.

Vinoteca García de la Navarra

Calle Montalbán 3, tel: 91 5233647; www.
garciadelanavarra.com; Mon 10am–5pm,

El Brillante serves a famous bocadillo de calamares

Tue–Sat 10am–5pm, 8.30pm–midnight; €€
Pedro and Luis García de Navarra – chef and sommelier respectively – are the well-respected brothers behind this modern Spanish gastrobar and restaurant, which is so successful that they also opened La Taberna del Pedro next door. There is a wide selection of wines by the glass.

Viridiana
Calle Juan de Mena 14; tel: 91 5234478; www.restauranteviridiana.com; Mon–Sun 1.30–4pm, 8.30pm–midnight; €€€€
Abraham García has been at the helm at Viridiana for 40 years and is a legendary figure in gastronomic circles. He was creating fusion dishes long before it became fashionable and Viridiana (named after the 1961 Buñuel film) is one of the most renowned in Madrid.

Plaza de Santa Ana, Barrio de las Letras and Lavapiés

Bodega de los Secretos
Calle San Blas 4; tel: 91 4290396; Mon–Sat, 1.30–5pm, 8.30pm–midnight; Sun 1.30–5pm; €€
Hidden away on a quiet side street, the restaurant sprawls through a labyrinth of underground wine cellars dating back to the 17th century. Tables in romantic arched alcoves ensure privacy and there is a great menu of modern Spanish dishes.

Cebo
Hotel Urban, Carrera de San Jerónimo 34; tel: 91 7877780; www.hotelurban.com/#!es/ restauracion/restaurante-cebo-info; Tue–Sat 1.30–3.30pm, 8.30–10.30pm; €€€€
After working with Ferran and Albert Adrià, Aurelio Morales opened his own restaurant in 2016. Dazzling dishes might include tiny shrimp emerging from a spray of zingy citrus foam.

Chuka Ramen Bar
Calle Echegaray 9; tel: 640 651346; www. chukaramenbar.com; Tue 8.30–11.30pm, Wed–Sat 1.30–3.30pm, 8.30–11.30pm; €
Chuka mixes Japanese and Chinese cuisines to create an original menu that features bowls of tasty ramen noodles as well as gyozas and bao buns. Always packed so book ahead.

El Lacón
Calle Manuel Fernández y González 8; tel: 91 4296042; www.mesonellacon.com; €
This very popular bar off Plaza de Santa Ana is a good place to start a tapas crawl. Order a beer or a glass of wine and you are given a complimentary tapa.

La Fisna
Calle Amparo 91; tel: 91 5395615; www.lafisna.com; Mon–Thu 11am–2pm, 7pm–midnight, Fri–Sat 12.30pm–midnight, Sun 12.30–5pm; €
A traditional bodega has been given a new lease of life after being taken over by wine lovers. There is a shop at the back, while the bar has a changing selection of at least 40 wines by the glass and good cheese and charcuterie as well as more elaborate tapas.

Taberna La Dolores is known for its selection of draft beers

La Sanabresa

Calle Amor de Dios 12; tel: 91 429 0338; Mon–Sat, 1–4.30pm, 8.30–11.30pm; €
The Sanabresa is a mad whirl of packed tables and rushing waiters. Most people have one of the bargain set menus, starting perhaps with garlic mushrooms followed by meatballs, hake or spare ribs. No booking but the queue moves fast.

La Venencia

Calle Echegaray 7; tel: 91 4297313; Mon–Sun 12.30am–3.30pm, 7.30pm–1am; €
One of the best-loved bars in Madrid, La Venencia is as stripped back as it gets, with just a wooden bar, barrels of sherry, faded posters on the walls and some tables at the back. Serving only several varieties of sherry and some basic tapas, it has been going since the 1930s and of course Hemingway was a regular.

Moharaj

Calle Ave María 18; tel 91 5272787; www.moharaj.com; Mon–Sun 1–5pm, 8pm–midnight; €
There are quite a few Indian restaurants to choose from on this hill in Lavapiés, but in-the-know locals rate Moharaj most highly. Most of the food is prepared to order. Try the prawns rezala, matar paneer and the lamb rogan josh.

Taberna de Antonio Sánchez

Calle Mesón de Paredes 13; tel: 91 5397826; www.tabernaantoniosanchez.com; Tue–Sat noon–midnight, Sun noon–4pm; €
Founded in 1830 by a matador, there is a bullfighting theme at this classic bar and restaurant, which has a zinc bar, marble tables, tiled walls and a bull's head on the wall. Have a draught vermouth, some tapas or a meal.

Taberna La Dolores

Plaza de Jesús 4; tel: 91 4292243; Mon–Sun 11am–12.30am, Fri–Sat until 1.30am; €
Pretty tavern with a tiled exterior that has been open for more than a century. It is known for its draught beer, so order a *caña* and a couple of *montaditos* – bread with tasty toppings – and soak in the atmosphere.

Triciclo

Calle Santa Maria 28; tel: 91 0244798; www.eltriciclo.es; Tue–Sun 1.30–4.30pm, 8.30pm–midnight; €€
The creative cuisine at Triciclo bar and restaurant is spiced up with a few fusion touches. It is very popular so book ahead and if it is full, try sister restaurant Tándem down the road at No. 39.

Chueca, Malasaña and Conde Duque

Angelita

Calle Reina 4; tel: 91 5216678; www.madrid-angelita.es; Mon 8.30pm–2am, Tue–Thu 1.30pm–2am, Fri–Sat 2pm–2.30am; €€
This gastrobar with lots of interesting wines by the glass has a daily-changing menu of dishes made with the best seasonal produce. The cocktail bar gets lively after midnight.

Bocaíto

Calle Libertad 6; tel: 91 5321219;
www.bocaito.com; Mon–Sun 12.30–4pm,
8pm–midnight, closed Sun evening; €€

This Andalusian tapas bar has been
open for more than 50 years. Friendly
old-school waiters stand behind the bar.
It is more fun to stand at the counter but
there is a restaurant section too.

Bodega de la Ardosa

Calle Colón 13; tel: 91 5214979;
www.laardosa.es; Mon–Fri 8.30am–2am,
Sat–Sun 8.30am–2.30am; €

With its red paintwork and smoked glass
sign, this is a truly Madrilenian place. You
either sit on stools around barrels or dive
under the bar to one of the secret tables
at the back. The tortilla is legendary, made
to the recipe of the owner's mother.

Bolívar

Calle Manuela Malasaña 28; tel: 91
4451274; www.restaurantebolivar.com;
Mon–Sat 1am–5.30pm, 8.30pm–1.30am; €€

Excellent produce coupled with a creative touch and slick service have made
this small restaurant a word-of-mouth
success. Inside it is all subtle stylishness
with a menu of creative classics, such as
the sirloin with foie in a Port reduction.

Café Comercial

Glorieta de Bilbao 7; tel: 91 0882525;
http://cafecomercialmadrid.com; Mon–Sun
8.30am–2am; €

One of Madrid's greatest traditional
cafés, opened since 1887 and revamped
in 2017. Fortunately, the atmosphere
has survived and it is still a favourite
haunt of writers, actors and artists.

Celicioso

Calle Barquillo 19; tel: 91 5322899;
www.celicioso.es; Mon–Sun 9am–10pm; €

Following the success of their nearby bak-
ery (calle Hortaleza 3), Celicioso opened
a café in the Only You Boutique hotel.
There are gluten-free cakes, sandwiches,
burgers and salads, as well as juices and
smoothies, to eat in or take away.

La Dichosa

Calle Bernardo López García 11; tel: 91
5418816; http://ladichosa.es; Mon–Thu
7pm–midnight, Fri 7pm–1am, Sat 1–4pm,
8pm–1am; €

With its blue, black and white décor and
arty clientele, this gastrobar in the bohemian Conde Duque area brings a bit of
New York sassiness to Madrid. Check
out the blackboards for unusual wines by
the glass or try one of the draught artisan beers.

La Manduca de Azagra

Calle Sagasta 14; tel: 91 5910112;
www.lamanducadeazagra.com; €€€

Much of the produce at this well-de-
signed restaurant comes from the owner's village in Navarra, a region renowned
for its vegetables as well as its elegant
cuisine and wines. Try the cristal peppers
and the caramel 'Torrija'. Popular with
media people, this is a smart place with
superb food.

The traditional Café Gijón serves a fixed-price lunch

MUY. Placer en Conserva

Calle Amaniel 36; tel: 91 5595784;
www.facebook.com/pg/muyplaceren
conserva; Tue–Thu 7pm–1am, Fri–Sat
noon–4pm, 8pm–2am, Sun noon–5pm; €

With mismatched tables and white-brick walls, this small bar creates tasty salads from Spain's gourmet tinned produce. There is good charcuterie and cheese as well as interesting wines by the glass and craft beers.

Taberna La Carmencita

Calle Libertad 16; tel: 91 5310911;
www.tabernalacarmencita.es; Mon–Sun
9am–2am; €

Lorca and Neruda were once regulars at this pretty tiled restaurant in trendy Chueca, which opened in 1854. Now, it has a modern Spanish menu using a lot of organic produce. You can eat all day and it is handy for breakfast or coffee and cake in the afternoon too.

Plaza de España and Moncloa

Bar Casa Paco

Calle Altamirano 38; tel: 91 5432821; Mon–Sat 7am–11.30pm, Sat from 9am; €

This busy bar is open from breakfast time onwards and offers a good-value set lunch, but most people come for a wedge of one of their tortilla omelettes, which are stacked up along the counter for you to choose from.

Cuenllas

Calle Ferraz 3; tel: 91 5473133;
www.cuenllas.es; Mon–Sat 2–4pm,
9–11pm; €€

Cuenllas started out as a delicatessen in 1939 and 50 years later added a tapas bar and restaurant with excellent service. It is all about the quality of the produce here. The crab cannelloni and the *callos a la madrileña* are favourites.

La Casa de Valencia

Paseo del Pintor Rosales 58; tel: 91 5441747; www.lacasavalencia.es; Mon–Sun 1–4pm, 8.30–11.45pm, Sun lunch only; €€

Founded in 1975 opposite the Oeste park, the Casa de Valencia is the place to come for an authentic Valencian paella or other rice dish – with lobster, monkfish or vegetables perhaps. Order some shellfish or a salad to start and allow a couple of hours to enjoy your lunch.

La Sifonería

Calle Martín de los Heros 27; tel: 91 2240574; www.lasifoneria.com; Mon–Wed and Sun 1–5pm, 7pm–1am, Thu 1pm–1am, Fri–Sat 1pm–2.30am; €

Run by two brothers, this popular bar and restaurant is decorated with vintage soda siphons and has good Spanish as well as international dishes to share as well as a fixed-price lunch. The bar offers draught vermouth, wines by the glass and cocktails.

Punto Vegano

Calle Luisa Fernanda 27; tel: 91 2940840; Thu–Sun 2–5pm, 8–11.30pm; €

Run by a young Uruguayan couple, this vegan café near the Templo de Debod

Michelin-star quality at Ramon Freixa Madrid

serves tasty hot dishes, including home-made ravioli and quinoa burgers, as well as sandwiches, salads, cakes and juices.

Paseo de la Castellana and Salamanca

Café Gijón

Paseo de Recoletos 21; tel: 91 5215425; www.cafegijon.com; Mon–Sun 7.30am–1.30am; €

With red velvet banquettes and marble tables, the Gijón, which opened in 1888, is one of the few traditional cafés left in the city and is a key element of the city's literary heritage. As well as drinks and snacks, there is a fixed-price lunch.

DiverXO

Hotel NH Collection Eurobuilding, calle Padre Damián 23; tel: 91 6700766; http://diverxo.com; Tue–Sat 2pm–1am; €€€€

Dabiz Muñoz is the only chef in Madrid to have been awarded three Michelin stars. Eating at DiverXO is an astounding experience, with spectacular Asian-inspired food and a theatrical vibe. You need to book months ahead.

Gourmet Experience Serrano

El Corte Inglés; calle Serrano 52; tel: 91 4325490; www.elcorteingles.es/super mercado/aptc/gourmet-experience/serrano; Mon–Thu 10am–midnight, Fri–Sat 10am–2am, Sun 11am–midnight; €€

Eat food by Michelin-starred chefs at more affordable prices in this gourmet food court on the top floor of El Corte Inglés department store. Try StreetXo – a simpler version of DiverXo – or the Mexican cuisine at Cascabel, which is run by the Punto MX team. There is gourmet ice cream by the Roca brothers at Rocambolesc too.

Punto MX

Calle General Pardiñas 40; tel: 91 4022226; http://puntomx.es; Tue–Sat 1.30–3.30pm, 9–11.30pm; €€€€

Roberto Ruiz is the only chef in Europe to gain a star for a Mexican restaurant and the only one in the world for a place serving purely Mexican cuisine. You need to book well in advance but you can also eat at the bar upstairs, which serves mezcal cocktails.

Ramon Freixa Madrid

Hotel Único, calle Claudio Coello 67; tel: 91 7818262; www.ramonfreixamadrid.com; Tue–Sat 1.30–3.30pm, 9–10.30pm; €€€€

Catalan chef Ramon Freixa has two Michelin stars at his glamorous restaurant, where the seasonally-changing menu might include Galician beef rib with mortadella and sea urchin. This is a great choice for a special occasion.

Sacha

Calle Juan Hurtado de Mendoza 11; tel: 91 3455972; Mon–Sat 1.30–4pm, 9pm–midnight; €€€

Consistently rated as one of the best restaurants in the city, Sacha was founded more than 40 years ago by the parents of the current owner and is renowned for its superb modern Spanish cuisine.

A performance of the opera Galanteos in Venice at the Teatro de la Zarzuela

NIGHTLIFE

Madrid is one of the liveliest cities in Europe after the sun goes down. With first-class cultural venues as well as bars and clubs to suit all tastes, you will never be stuck for something to do in the evening. The places recommended here are just a small selection of what is on offer, whether you want to see a flamenco show, go to a concert or dance the night away.

Opera, Zarzuela and Classical Music

Auditorio Nacional de Música
Calle Príncipe de Vergara 146; tel: 91 3370140; www.auditorionacional.mcu.es
The Auditorio Nacional is the home of the Orquesta y Coro Nacionales de España (National Orchestra and Choir of Spain).

With two main halls as well as smaller spaces, there are several concerts every day by Spanish and international orchestras and individual musicians.

Teatro Real
Plaza de Isabel II; tel: 91 5160660; www.teatro-real.com
Madrid's opera house is one of the most prestigious in the world, with a programme of events from September to June, featuring both its own and international productions. It is also a leading venue for classical music concerts and dance performances.

Teatro de la Zarzuela
Calle Jovellanos 4; tel: 91 5245400; http://teatrodelazarzuela.mcu.es
This charming 19th-century theatre is the home of zarzuela, the Madrid version of light opera, which is a mixture of a play and a musical, with a lot of humour thrown in. Most popular in the 19th century, the form is undergoing a bit of a revival.

Live Music

Clamores
Calle Alburquerque 14; tel: 91 4455480; www.salaclamores.es
Clamores specialises in jazz and blues but you might also hear flamenco, folk or tango. All sorts of artists and bands, from Spain and all over the world, perform at this atmospheric basement club in the Chamberí neighbourhood.

WiZink Center
Avenida Felipe II; tel: 91 4449949; www.wizinkcenter.es
This large venue in the Salamanca district, which most people still call by its original name of Palacio de Deportes, hosts music and sports events.

Sala La Riviera
Paseo Bajo de la Vírgen del Puerto; tel: 91 3652415; www.salariviera.es
Down by the Manzanares river, La Riviera is a landmark venue in Madrid. With two indoor spaces, a circular dance floor and

Flamenco at Cardamomo

a terrace, it is a late-night club as well as a place to see well-known international musicians.

Flamenco

Casa Patas

Calle Cañizares 10; 91 3690496; www.casapatas.com

Start the evening at this renowned flamenco centre with dinner in the Andalusian restaurant then go through to the back room for the live music and dance performances. Although undeniably touristy, the artists who perform here are top notch.

Cardamomo

Calle Echegaray 15; 91 8051038; www.cardamomo.es

Just about all the best contemporary flamenco musicians and dancers have appeared at this popular venue, including Estrella Morente and Antonio Carmona. There are usually three performances every evening, with various options for food and drinks.

Film

Golem

Calle Martín de los Heros 14; tel: 91 5593836; www.golem.es

There are several cinemas showing films in original version on and around calle Martín de los Heros, just off Plaza de España. Golem usually has at least six to choose from and has reduced prices on Mondays and Wednesdays, as well as Sunday evenings.

Cine Doré – Filmoteca Española

Calle Santa Isabel 3; tel: 91 3691125; www.mecd.gob.es/cultura-mecd/areas-cultura/cine/mc/fe/cine-dore

This Art Nouveau cinema was one of the first in Madrid and now houses the Filmoteca Española (Spanish Film Institute). As well as the programme of classic and avant-garde films, talks and other events, it has a café, bookshop and roof terrace.

Bars and Clubs

1862 Dry Bar

Calle Pez 27; 609 531 151; www.1862drybar.com

Run by top barman Alberto Martínez, this is a place for classic cocktails. Housed in a mid-19th-century palatial building, it is a good spot for a drink before or after dinner.

Museo Chicote

Gran Vía 12; tel: 91 5326737; http://grupo mercadodelareina.com/en/museo-chicote-en

This legendary cocktail bar has been attracting famous customers since the 1930s, including Ernest Hemingway, Salvador Dalí, Grace Kelly and Ava Gardner. While it now has more of a club vibe, the original Art Deco interior survives.

Marula Café

Calle Caños Viejos 3; 91 3661596; www.marulacafe.com

The funky soul vibe goes on till dawn at this club near Plaza de la Paja. There are different DJs every night and often there is a live band too.

Palm trees in Atocha Station

A–Z

A

Age Restrictions

The age of consent and the minimum age for marriage in Spain in 16. You must be 18 to drive a car and 21 to hire a vehicle. The legal age for buying and drinking alcohol is 18.

B

Budgeting

While not a cheap city, spending a few days in Madrid is not as expensive as other major European capitals.

Prices for food and drink do of course vary a lot from basic bars to smart places, but a small beer usually costs between €1.30 and €2. A glass of wine is normally from €1.80 to €4. Expect to pay around €1.50–2.50 for a coffee. A main course at an economic restaurant is around €10, while at a mid-range place – which is the norm in Madrid – €15–23 is normal. At a high-end restaurant, the price goes up to €25–40.

A room in a basic but adequate hotel costs around €60–80. Mid-range hotels tend to charge between €80 and €150. Deluxe hotels sometimes have surprisingly reasonable rates, starting from €150 and in most places the price does not exceed €350.

A taxi from the airport to the city centre costs €30, which is a flat rate. A single bus journey costs €1.50. The metro costs €1.50 for up to five stops and up to €2 for more than five stops. The useful 10-ride metrobus ticket costs €12.20 and is valid on the metro and bus. The Madrid Tourist Travel Pass, available from metro stations, includes metro, bus and local trains and is available for one to seven days, starting at €8.40 for one day (includes airport supplement).

The Paseo del Arte ticket (€29.60) allows admission to the Prado, Reina Sofía and Thyssen-Bornemisza museums and represents a saving of 20 percent compared to individual entrance tickets. It is available from the museums and their websites. The Five Museums: Another Madrid pass (€12) includes the Sorolla, Cerralbo, Lázaro Galdiano, Romanticism and Decorative Arts museums and is valid for 10 days.

C

Children

Spanish people adore children and they are made welcome just about everywhere, even in smart restaurants. Most hotels allow children under 12 to stay at no extra charge in existing beds. Cots are usually provided on request and babysitting can be arranged. Children

Metro sign

can travel free on public transport up to the age of four.

Clothing

While Madrilenians tend to be smartly dressed, it is fine to wear shorts around the city in warm weather, even in the evening, except for high-end restaurants. Ties are required for men in very few places. Informal clothes are usually okay for visiting churches, but women might want to take a scarf. In winter, take a hat and gloves as it can be very cold. In spring and autumn, you usually only need a light jacket.

Crime and Safety

Madrid is generally a safe city but petty crime is all too common. Try to keep important documents and valuables on your person rather than in a bag and only take what is absolutely necessary out with you. Be particularly vigilant on the metro (especially when travelling to and from the airport), at the Rastro street market and in busy areas such as the Puerta del Sol and the Gran Vía. At pavement cafés, keep bags on your lap with the strap around your wrist.

Customs

Travellers from EU countries may take unlimited goods for personal use into and out of Spain. This amount is regarded as up to 800 cigarettes, 10 litres of spirits and 90 litres of wine. Visitors may bring up to €10,000 into or out of the country without declaring it.

Tourists from outside EU countries can claim back IVA (value added tax) on purchases made in one store (ask for a tax-free form), and to a value of more than €90.16, at the Global Blue Refund Office at the airport.

Disabled Travellers

Madrid has improved its facilities for travellers with disabilities but there is still a long way to go. Most hotels have at least one adapted room, but it is worth checking the specifics beforehand. Most museums and sights are wheelchair accessible. All buses and 60 percent of the metro system are accessible. The Madrid tourist board website provides comprehensive information for visitors with disabilities with a downloadable booklet (www.esmadrid.com/en/accessible-madrid).

Electricity

The electrical current is 220 volts. There is no problem using 240 volt UK appliances. Sockets take round, two-pin plugs.

Embassies and Consulates

Many countries have embassies in Madrid, including the following:
Australia: Torre Espacio, Paseo de la Castellana 259d, tel: 91 3536600; www.spain.embassy.gov.au.

San Isidro festival is held on 15th May

Canada: Torre Espacio, Paseo de la Castellana 259d, tel: 91 3828400; www.canadainternational.gc.ca.

Ireland: Paseo de la Castellana 46; tel: 91 4364093; www.embassyorireland. es.

UK: Torre Espacio, Paseo de la Castellana 259d; tel: 91 714 6300; www.gov. uk/world/spain

United States: Calle de Serrano 75; tel: 91 5872200; http://madrid.us embassy.gov.

Emergencies

The Foreign Tourist Assistance Service, based at the police station (*comisaría de policia*) at calle Leganitos 19 (tel: 91 5488547), has multilingual staff to help tourists report crime and provide support with contacting family, banks etc. If you lose your passport, report it to the police and contact the relevant consulate or embassy to obtain an emergency document to enable you to travel. See also the Health section below.

Emergency services: dial 112 for police, ambulance and fire services. Multilingual operators are available.

Etiquette

If you are introduced to people by friends, it is usual to kiss lightly on both cheeks. If you are invited to someone's home, try to take a small gift, such as chocolates. It is normal to greet people in a lift. Spaniards do not usually share tables in bars and restaurants, even in fast-food and busy places.

F

Festivals

Carnaval. February–March. Celebrating the end of Lent, carnival involves processions, music, theatre, activities for children and fancy-dress parties. The most prestigious event is the spectacular masked ball at the Círculo de Bellas Artes.

Semana Santa. March–April. The processions during Easter week in Madrid are not as lavish as in other cities, but are still worth seeing – with the advantage that you do not have to fight your way through crowds.

Dos de Mayo. Early May. The Dos de Mayo festival, which lasts for at least a week, commemorates Madrid's battle against French troops on 2 May 1808 with a lively programme of arts events, pop concerts and street festivals, focused in the Malasaña area. 2 May is also the Day of the Madrid Region (www. madrid.org/fiestasdel2demayo).

San Isidro. 15 May is the feast day of San Isidro, the patron saint of Madrid, which is celebrated with much merriment in the streets of the most traditional areas and in the Pradera de San Isidro park. There are bullfights, concerts and other events on for at least two weeks around the main date (www. esmadrid.com/en/san-isidro).

Feria del Libro. Late May–early June. During the Madrid Book Fair around 200 bookshops have stalls in the Retiro Park.

Gay Pride Festival in Madrid is one of the largest in the world

There are signings and talks by dozens of leading Spanish and international authors and it is as much a social as a literary event (www.ferialibromadrid.com).

Suma Flamenca. June. Throughout June, there are performances by leading flamenco artists at large and small venues all over the city at this festival which is organised by the Madrid regional government (www.madrid.org/sumaflamenca).

PhotoEspaña. June–August. Photo-España is a major festival of photography and visual arts that takes place in cultural venues and outdoor locations across the city, with exhibitions, talks by leading photographers, courses, workshops, guided visits and a wealth of other activities (www.phe.es).

Los Veranos de la Villa. July–August. Throughout the summer, classical, rock and jazz concerts as well as theatrical and dance performances are staged at indoor and outdoor venues across the city, including the Sabatini gardens and the Casa de Campo park (www.veranos-delavilla.com).

Gay Pride. Late June–early July. Madrid hosts one of the biggest and most riotous Pride festivals in the world. Attracting thousands of people, this is one of the busiest times of the year in the city with street parties, concerts and parades (http://madridorgullo.com).

San Cayetano, San Lorenzo and La Paloma. 1–16 August. Madrid's most traditional street festivals, put on for locals rather than tourists, involve dressing up in traditional costume, dancing to live bands, alfresco eating and activities for all ages. Events take place along the sloping streets of the Austrias and Lavapiés neighbourhoods, the oldest and most characterful areas of the city (www.esmadrid.com/en/august-fiestas-madrid).

Gay and Lesbian Travellers

Madrid has one of the liveliest gay and lesbian scenes in Europe. The narrow streets of the Chueca neighbourhood are lined with bars, clubs and shops. This is also the hub of the Orgullo Gay, or Gay Pride festival – see Festivals above.

Health

The public health service is excellent and medical professionals usually speak good English. EU citizens are entitled to basic free medical treatment with the EHIC European Healthcard (www.ehic.org.uk). Take photocopies of the card and your passport as you will need to present both at a clinic or hospital. It is strongly advisable to take out private health insurance, whether you have the EHIC card or not.

If you have a medical emergency and need to go to hospital, the most central is the Hospital Clínico San Carlos in Moncloa (calle Profesor Martín Lagos; tel: 91 3303001). Look for the *Urgencias* (Accident and Emergency) department.

Pharmacists are thoroughly trained and can prescribe medication. Pharma-

Lunchtime at the Mercado San Miguel

cies are marked by a green neon cross and one in every district remains open all night and on holidays. The location and phone number of this *farmacia de guardia* is posted on the door of all the other pharmacies. All-night pharmacies can also be contacted by calling 098.

If you take prescription medication, ensure that you take extra supplies with you as Spanish chemists cannot accept foreign prescriptions. Given the dry climate and sun levels, it is a good idea to wear sunscreen and carry water with you in both summer and winter.

Tap water (*agua del grifo*) is excellent quality in Madrid and tastes fine. Although locals often drink bottled water, it is perfectly acceptable to ask for a glass or jug in bars and restaurants, even in smart places.

Hours and Holidays

Business hours vary a lot in Madrid, but many offices operate from 9am until 5pm or 6pm. It is becoming less common to have a long break for lunch but it is always advisable to try and get anything important done before 2pm. Most banks are open Monday to Friday from 8.30am to 2.30pm. Some branches also open on Saturday mornings. Most shops in the centre are open from 9.30am to 8.30pm, including on Sundays. Small shops outside the central area still close for lunch from 2pm until 5pm and often close on Saturday afternoons as well as all day on Sunday. Quite a few restaurants close on Sundays or Mondays.

Public Holidays

1 January *Año Nuevo*, New Year's Day
6 January *Día de Reyes*, Epiphany
19 March *San José*, St Joseph's Day (also Father's Day)
1 May *Fiesta de Trabajo*, Labour Day
2 May *Día de la Comunidad de Madrid*, Day of the Madrid Region
15 May *San Isidro* (patron saint of Madrid)
15 August *Asunción de la Virgen*, Assumption of the Virgin Mary
12 October *Día Nacional de España*, National Day of Spain, Columbus Day
1 November *Todos los Santos*, All Saints' Day
9 November *Nuestra Señora de la Almudena*, Our Lady of the Almudena (patron of Madrid)
6 December *Día de la Constitución Española*, Constitution Day
8 December *Día de la Inmaculada Concepción*, Immaculate Conception Day
25 December *Navidad*, Christmas Day
Movable dates: During Easter, between late March and mid-April, Maundy Thursday, Good Friday and Easter Sunday are public holidays. Easter Monday is a normal working day in Madrid.

Internet Facilities

As WiFi is available in most bars and restaurants – just ask for the password – internet cafés have largely disappeared but you can use computers at locutorios. Most hotels now provide WiFi. You

A well-stocked street kiosk

can connect free at the tourist office in the Plaza Mayor. The Centro Centro cultural centre in Plaza de Cibeles and the Círculo de Bellas Artes nearby have free WiFi and are comfortable places to sit if you need to do some work.

M

Media

Print media
The main national newspapers are *El País*, *El Mundo*, *ABC* and *La Vanguardia*. *El País* has an online English edition. All issue weekly cultural and entertainment listings' supplements, usually on Fridays. Kiosks on streets throughout the city often sell international as well as Spanish papers and magazines.

Radio
The Spanish national radio network, Radio Nacional de España, RNE (www.rtve.es/radio), has five main stations, covering news, classical music and modern music. The main commercial network is Cadena SER, with news and music channels. Madrid Live is a weekly English programme that covers cultural events in the city and is broadcast on the municipal M21 station (www.m21radio.es).

Television
The terrestrial national television channels are TVE 1 (La 1), TVE 2 (La 2) – from the state broadcaster RTVE – Antena 3, Tele 5, Cuatro and La Sexta. All have news bulletins plus lengthy chat, game and reality shows. Telemadrid focuses on news and events in the capital.

Money

Currency
The currency of Spain is the euro (€), which is made up of 100 cents. There are notes in denominations of 5, 10, 20, 50, 100 and 200. There are coins to a value of €1 and €2, as well as 50, 20, 10, five, two and one cents.

Credit cards
Cards are widely used and contactless payments are becoming standard. If you have to enter your pin number, you might be asked to show your passport, although this is becoming less common. It is normal to use cash for small amounts in bars and shops.

Cash machines
There are machines at banks all over the city, with instructions in English and other languages. Try to avoid taking out cash at night from a machine in the street. Most banks also have machines inside and there are also cash dispensers in El Corte Inglés department stores. There are two main systems, Telebanco and Servired, so if you have trouble with a machine, look for a cashpoint that uses the other system.

Traveller's cheques
These are not widely used but can be cashed at banks, Bureaux de Change

and major hotels. While you can use them in stores in tourist areas, traveller's cheques are not usually accepted in shops.

Tipping

There is no culture of leaving hefty tips in Spain. At high-end restaurants, leave 10 percent, but at most places around 5 percent is fine. It is normal but by no means compulsory to leave small change when paying for coffees, drinks or a taxi. At luxury hotels, however, international customs prevail.

Taxes

The standard rate of Value Added Tax (Impuesto de Valor Añadido, IVA) is 21 percent, but a reduced rate of 10 percent applies for hotel stays, bars, restaurants, cultural institutions and entertainment venues, including cinemas and theatres. It is usually – but not always – included in stated prices.

Post

Spain has a nationalised postal system, called Correos. There are surprisingly few post offices (*oficina de correos*) in Madrid, although stamps (*sellos*) are available at tobacconists (*estancos*). The main post office is on Plaza de Cibeles (Paseo del Prado 1) and there are post offices in El Corte Inglés department stores. Postboxes are yellow. A postcard or letter costs €1.45 to Europe and €1.80 to the US.

R

Religion

Roman Catholicism is the national religion in Spain and nearly 70 percent of citizens identify as such. St George's English Church (calle Nuñez de Balboa 43), part of the Church of England, is a diverse Christian community and holds services on Sundays. Muslims can worship at the mosque at the Centro Cultural Islámico de Madrid (calle Salvador de Madariega 4; www.centro-islamico.es). The Beth Yaacov synagogue is at calle Balmes 3.

S

Smoking

Smoking is not allowed in bars, restaurants, shops or other indoor public places or on public transport. Most hotels only allow smoking in designated rooms and many ban it altogether.

T

Telephones

The country code for Spain is 34. The local code for Madrid is 91 and this prefix must be dialled when you are in the city. To make an international call, dial 00 followed by the relevant country code. There are public phone boxes but it is often easier and cheaper to make international calls from a locutorio shop, where you can also buy phone cards. The main mobile operators are

The ceiling mosaic at the Almudena Cathedral

Movistar, Vodafone and Orange, with shops all over the centre. You can buy a pay-as-you-go phone or just a Spanish SIM card to use during your stay. As of 2017, roaming charges for customers within the EU have been abolished.

Time Zones

Spain is on Central European Time, which is one hour ahead of Greenwich Mean Time and British Summer Time. It is six hours ahead of New York.

Toilets

There are public toilets at some central points but they are a bit thin on the ground. Most bars will not mind if you go in to use the facilities but it is courteous to buy a coffee or a bottle of water. You can also pop into large hotels or museums, which usually have toilets in the lobby area. Look for an S (Señoras) or M (Mujeres) sign on the door for ladies' toilets and C (Caballeros) or H (Hombres) for the men's.

Tourist Information

The Madrid tourism organisation (www.esmadrid.com/en) has comprehensive practical and background information on its website. You can also consult the useful websites of the Madrid Region (www.turismomadrid.es) and the Spanish tourist office (www.spain.info) to plan your trip.

The main tourist office is at Plaza Mayor 27 (tel: 91 5787810). It has multilingual staff and is open every day of the year from 9.30am to 9.30pm. There are tourist information kiosks at key points around the city centre and at Terminal 2 and Terminal 4 at the airport.

Tours and Guides

It is a good idea to go on a tapas tour when you arrive, so that you know how and what to order for the rest of your stay. Devour Madrid (https://madrid-foodtour.com) has a range of options and knowledgeable, entertaining guides. Insider's Madrid (www.insidersmadrid.com) also offers excellent food tours as well as experiences such as visits to traditional shops and flamenco clubs. Madrid and Beyond (www.madridandbeyond.com) can organise all sorts of private specialist tours in the city and throughout Spain. Insight Guides offer a range of exciting and unique experiences in Madrid and beyond devised by local experts to your specifications (www.insightguides.com).

Transport

Arrival by Air

Adolfo Suárez Madrid-Barajas airport (www.aena.es) is 12km (7.5 miles) east of the city centre. There are three terminals in the original section plus the newer, separate Terminal 4, which handles Iberia and British Airways flights. Easyjet and Ryanair use Terminal 1.

There is a fixed €30 taxi fare to anywhere in the centre and the journey takes 20–30 minutes. The metro from the airport costs €1.50–2 plus a €3

Traffic on Gran Vía

supplement. You need to change lines at Nuevos Ministerios station to get to the centre, which is easy enough but obviously only advisable with manageable luggage.

The 24-hour Airport Express bus service, with luggage racks, costs €5 and takes 20–40 minutes, with stops at Plaza de Cibeles and Atocha station (www.emtmadrid.es/Aeropuerto). Route 200 on the municipal bus network goes from the airport to the Avenida de América transport hub and costs €1.50.

The C-1 local train (look for *Cercanías* signs) runs from Terminal 4 to the centre, stopping at Chamartin, Nuevos Ministerios, Recoletos and Atocha station, and costs €2.60 single.

Public Transport

Madrid has an efficient public transport system with extensive, easy to use metro and bus networks. See Budgeting above for fares and ticket information.

Metro

The metro system operates from 6am until 1.30am. There are 12 lines, covering the whole city. See www.esmadrid.com/en/madrid-metro and www.metromadrid.es/en for further information.

Bus

Buses run from 6am to 11.30pm. There is also an extensive night bus network through the nocturnal hours, which are known as *búhos* (owls) and leave from Plaza de Cibeles. You can buy a ticket from the driver or, if you have a 10-ride Metrobus ticket, punch it in the machine at the front of the bus.

Useful routes include No. 2, which goes through Plaza de España, Gran Vía and Plaza de Cibeles to the Retiro park, and No. 3, which goes along the calle Mayor, through Sol and up calle Hortaleza, between the Chueca and Malasaña neighbourhoods.

There are also two bus routes with just five seats that wiggle around the narrow streets of the centre. The M1 leaves from calle Alcalá at Sevilla metro station and heads south to La Latina, Tirso de Molina and Lavapiés, Madrid's most traditional areas. The M2 goes north from Sevilla up through bohemian Malasaña and Conde Duque to Argüelles, where there is an El Corte Inglés department store. See www.esmadrid.com/en/getting-around-madrid-by-bus and www.emtmadrid.es for more information.

Trains

The Cercanías rail network covers the Madrid region and is useful for day trips to El Escorial, Aranjuez and Alcalá de Henares (www.esmadrid.com/en/madrid-cercanias-train). For train travel around Spain, see www.renfe.com. The main stations are Chamartín in the north and Atocha in the south, with an underground rail link between the two.

The metro is a great way to get around the city

Taxis

Taxis are white with a red diagonal stripe on the sides and are plentiful and not too expensive – a short hop costs €5–10. A green light on the roof and a "Libre" sign show the vehicle is available. You can call a cab from Radio-Taxi (tel: 91 447 3232; www.radiotaxigremial.com) or Teletaxi (tel: 91 371 2131; www.tele-taxi.es). The Uber service also operates in Madrid, although the legal situation is constantly changing (www.uber.com/en-GB/cities/madrid).

Driving

There is no need to drive around central Madrid and parking can be difficult. Most sights are within walking distance or a few stops away by bus or metro. The minimum driving age is 18, seatbelts are compulsory and there are strict drink driving laws – the limit is 50mg of alcohol per 100ml of blood and just 25mg for drivers who have held a licence for less than two years. Driving is on the right.

Car Hire

You may want to hire a car to do some day trips. Rates are generally reasonable and bookings usually require a credit card. Be aware that the rental company might reserve a hefty deposit on your card. While the payment is not actually taken, you need to have sufficient credit available. The minimum age is 21. A national driver's licence is fine for EU citizens and usually for US citizens, but always check the conditions. Major companies have offices at the airport and train stations. Try Sixt (tel: 902 491 616; sixt.co.uk/car-hire/spain), Avis (tel: 902 180 854; avis.es) or Europcar (tel: 902 105 030; europcar.es/Madrid). Spanish companies National Atesa (tel: 902 100 101; www.atesa.es) and Pepe Car (tel: 902 996 666; www.pepecar.com) may be cheaper.

Visas and Passports

While visitors from countries that are part of the Schengen Agreement can enter Spain without a passport, everyone needs to carry a passport or identity card as it is a legal requirement in Spain and you will need to show identification at hotels and other places. For non-Schengen countries, EU nationals need to show their passport to enter Spain and visas are usually required by non-EU nationals unless their country has a reciprocal arrangement with Spain.

Weights and Measures

Spain uses the metric system.

Women Travellers

Women travelling alone should not encounter problems in Madrid and it is perfectly normal to eat on your own.

LANGUAGE

It is very useful and rewarding to learn some basic phrases in Spanish. English is widely spoken in shops and restaurants in tourist areas and in hotels and major museums, but is certainly not understood everywhere, particularly among older people.in Spanish.

As a general rule, the accent falls on the second-to-last syllable, unless it is otherwise marked with an accent (´) or the word ends in D, L, R or Z.

Vowels in Spanish are always pronounced the same way. The double L (LL) is pronounced like the y in 'yes', the double R is rolled. The H is silent in Spanish, whereas J (and G when it precedes an E or I) is pronounced like a guttural H (similar to the end sound of Scottish *loch*).

When addressing someone you are not familiar with, use the more formal 'usted'. The informal 'tú' is reserved for relatives and friends.

Basic Words and Phrases

yes *sí*
no *no*
thank you (very much) *(muchas) gracias*
you're welcome *de nada*
okay *bien*
please *por favor*
excuse me *perdóneme*
Can you help me? *¿Me puede ayudar?*
Do you speak English? (formal) *¿Habla inglés?*
Please speak more slowly *Hable más despacio, por favor*
I don't understand *No entiendo*
I'm sorry *Lo siento/Perdone*
I don't know *No lo sé*
No problem *No hay problema*
Where is...? *¿Dónde está...?*
I am looking for... *Estoy buscando*
That's it *Ese es*
Here it is *Aquí está*
There it is *Allí está*
Let's go *Vámonos*
At what time? *¿A qué hora?*
When? *¿Cuándo?*
here *aquí*
there *allí*

Greetings

Hello!/Hi! *¡Hola!*
Hello *Buenos días*
How are you? (formal/informal) *¿Cómo está?/¿Qué tal?*
What is your name? (formal) *¿Cómo se llama usted?*
Fine thanks *Muy bien, gracias*
My name is... *Me llamo...*
Mr/Miss/Mrs *Señor/Señorita/Señora*
Pleased to meet you *¡Encantado(a)!*
I am British/American *Soy británico/ norteamericano*
See you tomorrow *Hasta mañana*
See you soon *Hasta pronto*
Have a good day *Que tenga un buen día*
goodbye *adiós*
good afternoon/evening *buenas tardes*
good night *buenas noches*

Spoilt for choice

On Arrival

airport *aeropuerto*
customs *aduana*
train station *estación de tren*
platform *andén*
ticket *billete*
bus *autobús*
bus stop *parada de autobús*
metro station *estación de metro*
toilets *servicios*
taxi *taxi*

In the Hotel

I'd like a (single/double) room *Quiero una habitación (sencilla/doble)*
... with bath *con baño*
... with a view *con vista*
Does that include breakfast? *¿Incluye desayuno?*
lift/elevator *ascensor*
air conditioning *aire acondicionado*

Numbers

1 *uno*
2 *dos*
3 *tres*
4 *cuatro*
5 *cinco*
6 *seis*
7 *siete*
8 *ocho*
9 *nueve*
10 *diez*
11 *once*
12 *doce*
13 *trece*
14 *catorce*
15 *quince*
16 *dieciseis*
17 *diecisiete*
18 *dieciocho*
19 *diecinueve*
20 *veinte*
100 *cien*
1,000 *mil*
10,000 *diez mil*
1,000,000 *un millón*

Days of the Week

Monday *lunes*
Tuesday *martes*
Wednesday *miércoles*
Thursday *jueves*
Friday *viernes*
Saturday *sábado*
Sunday *domingo*

Seasons

Spring *primavera*
Summer *verano*
Autumn *otoño*
Winter *invierno*

Months

January *enero*
February *febrero*
March *marzo*
April *abril*
May *mayo*
June *junio*
July *julio*
August *agosto*
September *septiembre*
October *octubre*
November *noviembre*
December *diciembre*

Scene from Alejandro Amenábar's Open your Eyes

BOOKS AND FILM

From the books and plays of Golden Age writers to the films of Pedro Almodóvar, Madrid's literary and cinematic heritage is easily discoverable throughout the city and comes to life as you walk around its streets.

Around the Plaza de Santa Ana, you can see where Cervantes, Lope de Vega, Góngora, Moratín and other writers lived in the 16th, 17th and 18th centuries, which keeps their legacy very much alive. The Madrid of Benito Pérez Galdós, regarded as the Spanish Dickens or Balzac, is still recognisable around the Puerta del Sol too.

Pedro Almodóvar has showcased Madrid in most of his films, from the madness of the *movida madrileña* in *Labyrinth of Passions* in 1982 to the stylish modern city of *Julieta* in 2016. Other contemporary Spanish directors, such as Alejandro Amenábar, Álex de la Iglesia, Julio Medem, Cesc Gay and Jonás Trueba have depicted the city in very different and often alarming ways.

Books

Non-fiction

A Handbook for Travellers in Spain, by Richard Ford. Written in the mid-19th century, this is still one of the best books about Spain, with a fascinating section on Madrid.

A Traveller's Companion to Madrid, by Hugh Thomas. This gives a good histori-cal introduction, with excerpts from nov-els and journals from the 16th to the 20th centuries, including texts by George Bor-row, V.S. Pritchett and Ernest Hemingway.

Everything is Happening, by Michael Jacobs. This short book, which the acclaimed Hispanophile was working on when he died in 2014, explores the author's lifelong fascination with Veláz-quez's masterpiece *Las Meninas* and clearly shows his affection for Madrid.

Ghosts of Spain, by Giles Tremlett. This account of travelling through Spain in the early 21st century to understand the country through its history is an invalua-ble preparation for visiting the city.

Hotel Florida: Truth, Love and Death in the Spanish Civil War, by Amanda Vaill. Fascinating telling of the lives of Ernest Hemingway, Martha Gellhorn Robert Capa and Arturo Barea during the Civil War at the Hotel Florida, which stood on the Gran Vía.

Madrid: A Cultural and Literary History, by Elizabeth Nash. A well-written, enter-taining overview of how artists and writ-ers lived and worked in the city over the centuries.

Fiction

A Heart so White, by Javier Marías. This novel, as well as *Tomorrow in the Bat-tle Think On Me* and some of his other books, is partly set in Madrid and evokes an intriguing image of the city. Marías is

Cult classic Women on the Verge of a Nervous Breakdown

widely regarded to be the greatest living Spanish writer.

Don Quixote, by Miguel de Cervantes. Walking around the Barrio de las Letras might inspire you to read the greatest Spanish novel about the travels of the errant knight – which is fortunately also available in English.

Fortunata and Jacinta, by Benito Pérez Galdós. This is one of the greatest works of Spanish literature, about life in Madrid in the late-19th century. Several other novels by Galdós are also available in English, including *The Spendthrifts* and *Miau*.

Leaving the Atocha Station, by Ben Lerner. The debut novel by the renowned American writer, published in 2011, skewers the pretentiousness of foreigners in Madrid while also amusingly describing the city in the early 21st century.

Madrid Tales, edited by Helen Constantine. This collection of stories, translated by Margaret Jull Costa, is the perfect companion for a stay in the city. With pieces by Benito Pérez Galdós, Javier Marías and Elvira Lindo, amongst other leading Spanish authors, the stories guide you through the history, geography and social life of the city.

The Beehive, by Camilo José Cela. The classic novel by Nobel prize-winner Cela is a vivid portrayal of life in Madrid in the 1940s. The book was made into a film in 1982.

The Forging of a Rebel, by Arturo Barea. Based on Barea's own life, this trilogy gives an insight into the turbulent situa-tion in Madrid in the first half of the 20th century.

Winter in Madrid, by C.J. Sansom. This absorbing novel about a British spy gives a vivid picture of the desperate situation in Madrid after the Civil War.

Films

Julieta (2016). Walk along calle Fernando VI and you will recognise the locations of some of the scenes from Almodóvar's mesmeric film.

Open your Eyes (1997). Worth seeing for the sight of a deserted Gran Vía alone, Alejandro Amenábar's film was remade as *Vanilla Sky* by Tom Cruise.

Sex and Lucía (2001). Julio Medem's erotic film is set partly in Madrid and the main character lives in a traditional apart-ment on the Plaza de las Comendadoras.

The Day of the Beast (1996). Alex de la Iglesia's anarchic comedy blazes a cha-otic trail through Madrid in a search for the devil at Christmas.

The Flower of My Secret (1995). Alm-odóvar is at his best in this film, which captures the magic of Madrid and was shot in the Plaza Mayor and around Plaza de los Carros and Plaza de Callao.

The Quince Tree Sun (1992). This doc-umentary film by poetic filmmaker Víc-tor Erice follows the great artist Antonio López as he creates a painting.

Women on the Verge of a Nervous Breakdown (1988). Almodóvar's glori-ous romp through Madrid shows the city as its zaniest, with locations featuring the Jerónimos and Chamberí areas.

ABOUT THIS BOOK

This *Explore Guide* has been produced by the editors of Insight Guides, whose books have set the standard for visual travel guides since 1970. With top-quality photography and authoritative recommendations, these guidebooks bring you the very best routes and itineraries in the world's most exciting destinations.

BEST ROUTES

The routes in the book provide something to suit all budgets, tastes and trip lengths. As well as covering the destination's many classic attractions, the itineraries track lesser-known sights, and there are also excursions for those who want to extend their visit outside the city. The routes embrace a range of interests, so whether you are an art fan, a gourmet, a history buff or have kids to entertain, you will find an option to suit.

We recommend reading the whole of a route before setting out. This should help you to familiarise yourself with it and enable you to plan where to stop for refreshments – options are shown in the 'Food and Drink' box at the end of each tour.

For our pick of the tours by theme, consult Recommended Routes for… (see pages 6 – 7).

INTRODUCTION

The routes are set in context by this introductory section, giving an overview of the destination to set the scene, plus background information on food and drink, shopping and more, while a succinct history timeline highlights the key events over the centuries.

DIRECTORY

Also supporting the routes is a Directory chapter, with a clearly organised A–Z of practical information, our pick of where to stay while you are there and select restaurant listings; these eateries complement the more low-key cafés and restaurants that feature within the routes and are intended to offer a wider choice for evening dining. Also included here are some nightlife listings, plus a handy language guide and our recommendations for books and films about the destination.

ABOUT THE AUTHORS

Annie Bennett writes about Spanish travel, food and culture for national newspapers and magazine in the UK and beyond. When not travelling around Spain, she divides her time between Madrid and the Gower coast in South Wales.

CONTACT THE EDITORS

We hope you find this Explore Guide useful, interesting and a pleasure to read. If you have any questions or feedback on the text, pictures or maps, please do let us know. If you have noticed any errors or outdated facts, or have suggestions for places to include on the routes, we would be delighted to hear from you. Please drop us an email at hello@insightguides.com. Thanks!

CREDITS

Explore Madrid
Editor: Carine Tracanelli
Author: Annie Bennett
Head of Production: Rebeka Davies
Update Production: Apa Digital
Picture Editor: Tom Smyth
Cartography: Carte
Photo credits: Alamy 7M, 19, 36, 44, 61, 63, 64/65, 66, 67, 68/69, 73, 76/77, 103, 104, 120, 121; Alex Segre/REX/Shutterstock 49, 102; AWL Images 1, 4/5T, 8/9T, 26/27T; Corrie Wingate/Apa Publications 6TL, 7MR, 8ML, 8MC, 8MC, 8MR, 8MR, 12, 13T, 12/13T, 14B, 31, 38, 46, 53L, 54, 55L, 54/55, 79, 80, 81L, 80/81, 85, 86, 87M, 87T, 86/87T, 98, 99, 108, 109; Derby Hotels Collection 88ML, 95, 100; Getty Images 7T, 10, 16, 16/17, 20T, 37, 39, 42, 51, 52/53, 60, 62, 64, 65L, 107; iStock 4ML, 4MC, 4MR, 4MR, 4MC, 4ML, 6BC, 8ML, 11, 13MC, 14/15T, 18, 20B, 21, 23, 26MR, 26ML, 26MC, 26ML, 28/29, 32/33, 34, 34/35, 40/41, 43, 45, 48, 56, 57, 58/59, 68, 69L, 70, 75, 82, 110, 111, 112, 113, 114, 115, 116, 117, 118, 119; Leonardo 88MR, 88MR, 88MC, 88/89T, 90, 91, 96, 97, 105; Mandarin Oriental Hotel Group Limited 94; Meliá Hotels 92; Museo Thyssen-Bornemisza 47L; Oscar Gonzalez/NurPhoto/REX/Shutterstock 106; Palladium Hotel Group 88ML, 88MC, 93; Public domain 6MC, 24/25, 26MR, 30, 50, 77L; Shutterstock 6ML, 7MR, 22, 26MC, 52, 71, 72, 76, 78, 83, 84; Starwood Hotels & Resorts 46/47; SuperStock 17L, 35L, 74, 101
Cover credits: iStock (main&bottom)

Printed in Poland

First Edition 2018

Every effort has been made to provide accurate information in this publication, but changes are inevitable. The publisher cannot be responsible for any resulting loss, inconvenience or injury.

DISTRIBUTION

UK, Ireland and Europe
Apa Publications (UK) Ltd
sales@insightguides.com
United States and Canada
Ingram Publisher Services
ips@Ingramcontent.oom
Australia and New Zealand
Woodslane
info@woodslane.com.au
Southeast Asia
Apa Publications (Singapore) Pte
singaporeoffice@insightguides.com
Hong Kong, Taiwan and China
Apa Publications (HK) Ltd
hongkongoffice@insightguides.com
Worldwide
Apa Publications (UK) Ltd
sales@insightguides.com

SPECIAL SALES, CONTENT LICENSING AND COPUBLISHING

Insight Guides can be purchased in bulk quantities at discounted prices. We can create special editions, personalised jackets and corporate imprints tailored to your needs.
sales@insightguides.com
www.insightguides.biz

INDEX

MAP LEGEND

● Start of tour	━━━ Railway	M̂ Museum/gallery
⇥ Tour & route direction	🚌 Main bus station	⚙ Theatre
❶ Recommended sight	℗ Car park	🏰 Castle
❷ Recommended restaurant/café	Ⓜ Metro station	▦ Important building
★ Place of interest	⊠ Main post office	▨ Park
❶ Tourist information	⚊ Monument	▢ Urban area
✈ Airport	⛪ Church	▢ Non-urban area
	✡ Synagogue	▦ Transport hub